Relevance of Political Theory

Relevance of Political Theory

L.S. Rathore

MPISSR
Madhya Pradesh Institute of Social Science Research, Ujjain

RAWAT PUBLICATIONS
Jaipur • New Delhi • Bangalore • Hyderabad • Guwahati

ISBN 81-316-0364-4

Published by
Prem Rawat for **Rawat Publications**
Satyam Apts., Sector 3, Jawahar Nagar, Jaipur 302 004 (India)
Phone: 0141 265 1748/7006 Fax: 0141 265 1748
E-mail: info@rawatbooks.com
Website: www.rawatbooks.com

New Delhi Office
4858/24, Ansari Road, Daryaganj, New Delhi 110 002
Phone: 011 2326 3290

Also at *Bangalore, Hyderabad* and *Guwahati*

Typeset by Rawat Computers, Jaipur
Printed at Chaman Enterprises, New Delhi

Dedicated to

(Late) Professor S.C. Dube

for his outstanding contribution to
the field of Social Sciences

Contents

Preface

I am extremely grateful to Professor S.C. Dube, who had invited me to deliver a series of lectures under the auspices of the Madhya Pradesh Uchcha Shiksha Anudaan Aayog. Prof Dube was a renowned sociologist of international repute and, as such, this book has been dedicated to him in appreciation of the services rendered by him to the cause of the development of sociology and allied disciplines. I cannot conceive of any better method of felicitating a scholar of such outstanding eminence as Prof Dube than to dedicate this book to him.

The Madhya Pradesh Uchcha Shiksha Anudaan Aayog was kind enough to permit me to deliver these lectures at the School of Studies in Political Science, Vikram University, Ujjain (MP). Prof R.S. Gautam, the then professor and head of the School of Studies in

Political Science, took special care to arrange these lectures in a most befitting manner. I am, indeed, very thankful to him.

I must acknowledge my thanks to Dr P.S. Bhati, retired professor of Political Science, University of Jodhpur, and Prof B.R. Purohit, who extended all help during the preparation of the manuscript and reading the proofs.

I am also grateful to the chairperson of the Madhya Pradesh Institute of Social Science Research, Ujjain, for showing interest in this project and getting this book published and that, too, with such skill and precision. My thanks are also due to Pranit Rawat, Rawat Publications, Jaipur, for bringing out this book and for the cover design. The secretarial assistance rendered by Sudeep Mishra of MPISSR, Ujjain, deserves all praise.

L.S. Rathore

1

The Disagreements and Controversies in Political Theory

Political theory has a hoary historical past. It is more than 2,300 years old. It has often sprung from incongruous and heterogeneous sources and even been seeded and nourished by other branches of knowledge. From the days of the Greeks to the present day, it has moved or flowed through luscious meadows and thorny paths, sunny days and weedy gloom, and periods of both fructification and decay. Its birth was characterized by Plato's idealism and Aristotle's rationalism—two most powerful currents that have often been interpreted, tossed and twisted by the political thinkers of later ages. The elevated idealism of Plato and the scientific methodology of Aristotle have been a considerable source of inspiration, debate and even wrangles among political thinkers through the ages. Since the days of the Greeks, the settings of political theory have altered often, the emphases have moved back and forth, and the terms used have changed their meanings, until sometimes, they bear almost the opposite of their original significance.[1] The lack of consensus as to political theory's meaning and its varieties—often overlapping—make the task of delivering lectures on political theory a difficult and intricate one. So many hands have helped in developing political theory's myriad forms and shapes that, today, its corpus has many 'odd-shaped humps and bumps'.[2] It is in a state of considerable confusion, for not only are the matters which it discusses of a highly controversial nature, but there is disagreement both as to the character of its central problems and as to the appropriate methods of treating them.[3] There is no systematic evolution in its development, no logical continuum, and its amorphous contours are often shifting, even radically changing, boundaries. It has passed through various odysseys and periods of glorification and depression, of turmoil and conflict, of political and social crises, and of pessimism and confidence. Its corpus is cluttered with a large and diverse number of political theorizers, coming from different walks of life. Its myriad forms and shapes are the result of contributions from kings, philosophers, popes, saints, political leaders, rogues and highwaymen of every sort, stripe and denomination. Plato was a philosopher; Aristotle was a biologist as well as a philosopher; St Augustine was a bishop; Thomas Hobbes was a tutor of the royal family; Rousseau was an essayist and a novelist; Herbert Spencer was an engineer and inventor; Descartes was a mathematician; Charles Darwin was a naturalist; John Locke was a physician; Montesquieu was a judge; T.H. Green was a sober realist and a soaring idealist; John Stuart Mill was a high official of the British East India Company; Spinoza made his living by polishing lenses; Voltaire, the finest ornament of France, started as a playwright; Immanuel Kant, who never left his native city, was a university teacher; H.J. Laski was a politician and a theorist; Karl Marx was an economist; and Lenin was an action oriented leader and agglomerator of ideas. In the modern period, John Dewey and Bertrand Russell were philosophers; J.A. Hobson and Friedrich Hayek were economists; Max Weber and Emile Durkheim were sociologists; Sigmund Freud and Erich Fromm were psychologists; T.S. Eliot and Aldous Huxley were literary men; Vilfredo Pareto and Georges Sorel were engineers; Hitler and Mussolini were men in power; Gandhi and Thoreau were saints and Stalin and Mao Tse-tung were pathfinders who could boast of discovering the basic laws of the universe. Political theory, thus, has sprung from heterogeneous sources and its dimensions are complex and scattered.

Political theory has always been seeded and nourished by other branches of knowledge. Its traditional bases have been history, philosophy, ethics, geography and related social sciences. In recent years, there has been a formidable invasion of its terrain by sociology and psychology. The contemporary onslaught of mathematics, statistics, biology, cultural anthropology and economics has conspicuously altered and twisted its frontiers. As a result of the massive invasions of varied disciplines on the unprotected fortress of political theory, the boundary lines between political theory and other disciplines have grown less distinct, as a result of which it seems that the writings on political theory follow fashion. Consequently, the literature of political theory has adopted new styles, themes and goals, similar to the changes that occur in women's fashions from time to time. These fashions are the product of historical events, wars and social upheavals, periods of depression and agony, the desire of superpowers for domination and the centrifugal tendencies of a multi-polar world, and the remarkable advances in technology and computer science, which have produced political theories and ideological movements of an unprecedented character. So many scholars from diverse walks of life and so many conflicting ideas and ideologies sprawl over the field of political theory, that it is hardly possible to explore and locate its exact parameters. It is apparent, thus, that political theory is coiled and ensnared in a web of serious challenges and problems of gigantic magnitude.

There are acrimonious debates and endless wrangles even about the definition and value of political theory. One observer considers political theory to be inseparable from political thought. Another contends that it cannot be distinguished from philosophy. A third points out the necessity of analytically separating it from philosophy and ideology. A fourth suggests that it is the most encompassing type of intellectual activity and classifies thought, philosophy and ideology as specific forms of theory. A fifth contends that statements about historical events ought to be included in the subject matter of political theory. A sixth emphasizes that its subject matter is amenable to scientific analysis. A seventh is strongly concerned with value presuppositions. An eighth states that it is a systematic analysis of political relations. A ninth considers theory as a search for political wisdom. A tenth refutes it by saying that theory is not knowledge, but a necessary tool on the road to knowledge. An eleventh would prefer to refer to it as an interpretation or crystallization of a point of view.

Answers of an extreme nature have been given frequently about the value of political theory. One is that political theory has no value; it is arid, abstract and dull. Another is that it is damnably dangerous, dealing with darkness and devoted like the devil to disaster. A third states that sensibly handled with a commonsense attitude to the real values of social life, political theory is both concrete and a fruitful study. And a fourth asserts that it contains the distilled wisdom of ages, essential for the establishment of a just order. Thus, the controversy over the academic credentials of its definition and value has introduced massive confusions in the realm of political theory.

Further, thinkers and philosophers rarely agree on the subdivisions of political theory. One lays emphasis on its ethical field, dealing with what ought to be and employing the rationalistic, deductive method. Another prefers its speculative dimension, which consists of imaginative constructions of ideal or utopian states. A third sticks to sociological subdivisions, studying the state as a form of social organization in relation to society as a whole, and using the empirical method. A fourth adopts the legal or juristic subdivision, dealing with the nature of laws, sovereignty and constitutions. A sixth unfolds its scientific field, seeking to extract generalizations, trends and laws, gathered from dates, observations, measurement and analysis. And a seventh divides it according to its chronological development. These diversified opinions as to its subdivisions have led to an increasing fragmentation of political theory in recent years. Its antiquity, confused paternity, overlapping trends and tangents, the rich variety of its components and the quest for rigorous methodology have introduced a kind of theoretical bewilderment in political theory and it is well nigh impossible to delineate its subdivisions neatly and precisely.

Politics, today, is full of ideas and theories. The idea of politics includes the notion of government as a social function of political activity and the notions of power and influence, both as individual and group goals and as the means whereby decisions are made and enforced. But the definitions diverge sharply when one questions the purposes of the rules and what kind of power and influence are characteristically 'political'. One writer calls the object of rule making the creation of 'the good life' for a society. A second sees its object as 'a life of moral perfection'. A third lays emphasis on 'the realization of human freedom'. A fourth attempts to combine the concepts of 'freedom' and 'goodness' in his vision of the purpose of political life. And a fifth is satisfied simply with order or control as the end of political activity.

Similarly, there are many views about the characteristics of political influence. To the Greeks, it meant government by pure persuasion and they spoke of force in governing as a 'pre-political' phenomenon. In contrast, Treitschke, a nineteenth century philosopher, spoke of war and violence as 'politics in the highest degree'. A contemporary writer, Heinz Eulau, says that 'what makes a man's behaviour political is that he rules and obeys, persuades and compromises, promises and bargains, coerces and represents, fights and fears'. One group of writers stresses the cooperative and harmonious aspects of political activity, others emphasize rivalry and conflict. Political theories, one must remember, have been associated with diverse purposes. One writer has associated theories with the 'public government'. A second prefers to study 'small groups'. A third wants to explore the nature of the good, best, right or rational order. For a fourth, it has the character of a logical construct, developed from empirical data, but not identical with any observable political system. A fifth is engaged in an endless wrangle over the ethical or purely technical character of theory. And a sixth claims the field of 'political choice' as relevant for a theorist. This diversification in the application of political theory is a subject of never ending disharmony and conflicting answers.

Adding to this is the overwhelming interest of our generation in politics. A man may decide that he is uninterested in poetry and art, or in chemistry and mathematics, and no one may be the loser save himself, nor will anyone trouble him. But, although a man may decide that he is uninterested in politics and may prefer to have the provincial mind, the practice of politics will not be uninterested to him, whether in peace or in war. If he will not pull his weight, he will most certainly be pulled. This ever expanding field of politics has considerably altered the meaning attached to the term 'politics', which, in turn, has intensified controversies in political theory. The study of politics and its processes are no longer clothed in traditional garments. The traditional contours of politics in terms of governments, states, sovereignty and authority appear narrow and restrictive. A host of theorists have interpreted politics in a new fashion: 'Politics is the authoritative allocation of values'[4]; 'Politics is who gets what, when and how'[5]; 'Politics is an activity by which an issue is agitated or settled'; 'Politics is the struggle for power'[6]; 'Politics is a systematic effort to move other men in the pursuit of other design'[7]; 'Politics is the study of social relationships and of the human (and even non-human) social structure' and 'it is identical with sociology'[8]; or 'The central problem in politics is the management of conflict'. It is this new interpretation of politics that has drastically altered the parameters of political theory. Although these definitions of politics are not self-contained, they have been able to throw up many more theories and generalizations. Lured by the new meanings attached to 'politics', many contemporary political theorists boldly proclaim that theory is not knowledge, "it is only a tool. And like all tools, it tends periodically to wear out and need replacement." The new meaning of politics has accelerated theorists' attention on the 'observed and observable' behaviour of men. It argues that political theory should seek self-evident, immediate, objective, analytical and explanatory knowledge. It has even listed 'policy science' as another variety of political theory. As such it is difficult to derive the exact meaning of political theory from the labyrinth of definitions that have cropped up, like mushrooms, in the contemporary period.

The interests, angles and commitments of political theorists have been different. *Theories of the Political System,* written by a contemporary writer, William T. Bluhm, has shown renewed interest in the great theorists of the past. C.B. Macpherson, in his *Political Theory of Possessive Individualism,* has forcefully set out the argument for the unstated, tacit assumptions that underlie a theory or the events that form the backdrop of a theorist's work. The interest of Sir Ernest Barker's *Principles of Social and Political Theory* (1951) has been a search for an end oriented State, or the good at which the State should aim. The concern of A.J. Ayer's *Language, Truth and Logic* (1936) has been to set forth the verification criteria by which the meaning of a proposition is assured by its method of verification, or to conclude that if a proposition is not amenable to verification by empirical demonstration, it is meaningless. H.J. Laski's *A Grammar of Politics* contains many statements and propositions regarding what the State ought to do. T.D. Weldon's *Vocabulary of Politics* (1953) presents an extreme expression of the logical positivist position with regard to political theory. Thomas L. Thorson's *Logic of Democracy* aims to show that there is a middle way between the extremes of Weldon's subjectivism on the one hand and the transcendental objective values of a writer like Plato on the other. A much more rigorous approach is to be found in *Political Argument* by Brian Barry, a work examining the nature of political evaluation and the role of principles, combining sophisticated analytical philosophy with the refined analysis of economics and games theory. The classical philosophy of history, as contained in the theories propounded by St Augustine, has received trenchant attacks in *The Poverty of Historicism* and *Historical Inevitability,* written by Karl Popper and Sir Isaiah Berlin, respectively. T.H. Green's *Principles of Political Obligation* offers a complex account of the concept of political obligation. S.I. Benn and R.S. Peters, in their valuable work, *Social Principles and the Democratic State,* prefer to expound the principle of equality. Still other writers lay emphasis on the commitment to concepts such as freedom, property, majority rule, consent, law, liberty, morality and so on. One can, therefore, say that since the interests, emphases and commitments of political theorists have been different, political theory has never been able to acquire an agreed shape or a specific mould and it should not struggle to have one.

Again, a bewildering maze of theoretical styles in the contemporary period have introduced the worst kind of blockage in the realm of political theory, so much so that its arena has become dim, hazy and overlapped. The tradition of the Chicago School has declined. Similarly, under the debris is the critical theory of the Frankfurt School, the radical sociology of C. Wright Mills, the symbolic interactionism of G.H. Mead, and the philosophy of pragmatism of John Dewey. While structural functionalism dominated the scene during the 1940s and 1950s, it had to bow down before the conflict theory alternative. The conflict theory (1956) was little more than a mirror image of structural functionalism with little intellectual integrity of its own. The upsurge of Peter Blau's exchange theory (1950s) and Erving Goffman's dramaturgical analysis (focus on actors, actions and interactions) proved short-lived. In the 1960s and 1970s, there was a boom in creative sociology, which includes the phenomenological, ethnomethodological and existential theories. The systems theory has witnessed both a meteoric rise and a meteoric fall. The much heralded style of 'biopolitics' is full of cracks and clefts. The point is that political theories have been proliferating in number, style and range in recent years, but many of these are little more than brief bursts of theoretical activity, which sank naturally in a relatively short span of time.

Scientific political theory has been going through a crisis of unprecedented magnitude in this century and is still in the midst of it. Its foundations, methods, uses, strengths and limitations—even its wisdom—are being questioned. Its marked trend towards methodological awareness and scientific value relativism has not been able to verify the ultimate principles of right and wrong, of just and unjust. Its lack of clarity on its objectives has been its weakness. Its scientific relativism has been branded as a kind of 'obvious absurdity'. Its rebels can be classified roughly into two groups—'those who have tried to get around scientific relativism without refuting it and those who have attempted to refute it'.[9] The first group has been called 'professional escapees' and some of its writers have taken typical routes of refuge in religion, assumptions, references to general agreement, constitution, traditions and the history of political ideas; others have chosen to escape into the fields of biology, psychology and psycho-analysis, or to refer for knowledge of values to intuition. The second group consists of those writers who have been impassioned, impatient and have even refuted outright scientific value relativism. The attempts to knock down scientific relativism have generally taken one of several distinct paths. One writer has rejected the methodological distinction between facts and values and said that scientific method cannot lead to absolute statements on the hierarchy of values. A second writer has attacked it from the angle of inconsistency and said that its principles, standards, criteria and generalizations are merely 'procedural means' and that they are no more than 'intellectual instruments' in our inquiry. A third says that scientific judgement is, in the ultimate analysis, always a moral judgement. A fourth view is that of the Neo-Thomists, who urge us to return to the scholastic concept of science, which includes supra-empirical and supra-rational kinds of wisdom. Its leading exponent was the French philosopher, Jacques Maritain. Maritain says, "What misery it is for the mind to reduce science to a type of empiro-logical science, that is, the physico-mathematical sciences and the sciences of phenomena." There 'must' be such a non-empirical science, he exclaims, some knowledge in which the intellect is 'on the inside'. He laments that metaphysics has been wrongly ousted from science; he speaks of the 'mystery of abstract intuition'. This call for the re-inclusion of metaphysics in science has also been echoed by Eric Voegelin, who was not a Thomist. He calls for a 'restoration' of political science and for its 're-theorization' through a revival of the attempts made by the Greek philosophers and the medieval Christian scholars to provide an ontological description of the order of values, 'the theoretical orientation of man in his world, the great instrument for man's understanding of his own position in the universe'. This aim, he argues, cannot be reached by scientific method and, as such, we should free ourselves from the positivistic approach. A fifth considers that, at least in cultural questions, one should renounce the insistence on 'scientific dignity'. A sixth claims that truth can be found through intuition, which is true knowledge, or 'inward seeing'. Against the position taken by the 'rebels' of the scientific method is the stand in favour of the scientific method, to which I shall turn later. This endless wrangle over the pros and cons of the scientific method has introduced a very real dilemma in political theory.

The crisis in political theory is also due to the unsettled use of terms such as 'philosophy', 'science', and 'theory'. The interrelationship between philosophy, science and theory is one of the fundamental problems in the present predicament of scientific thinking. Of course, there is no complete disagreement about the use of the three terms, but divergences do prevail. A theory may be an attempt to explain or may refer to some general law or may consist of a suggestion or a legal, moral, aesthetic or procedural norm. Similarly, philosophy has had many different meanings in the history of ideas. Originally, its meaning was all inclusive and coextensive with that of science—it implied a universalistic reference. It tries to explain, not something, but everything—the universe, the macro cosmos and the micro cosmos. Others emphasize its speculative dimensions, and some would prefer to explain phenomena through philosophy, whereas those who plead for precision and control in science prefer to distinguish between science and philosophy. The entire development has led to two antagonistic cross-currents of thought. One school tries to make philosophy more fully 'scientific' and the second school proposes to liberate science from its narrow rules and make it 'philosophic' once more, so as to include metaphysics. Both of these movements, however, run clearly counter to the use of the terms, philosophy and science. They have introduced ambiguity and even blurred the dimensions of theory, philosophy and science.

The contradictions and controversies in political theory have increased abundantly during the post-war period. Vigorous challenges have been issued to the legitimacy of its theoretical enterprise, but simultaneously, claims that it is legitimate enterprise have been made insistently. One school speaks about the 'demise' of political theory. Another proclaims its 'revival'. A third styles behaviouralism as one of the most important developments in political science. A fourth characterizes behaviouralism as simply a 'mood', rather than a precisely defined mode of inquiry. A fifth advocates that most vital knowledge is philosophical and that the central concern in political theory is the moral evaluation of political power. A sixth posits that value free political theory is hardly possible and accuses behaviouralists of concentrating on pseudo-politics while neglecting real politics. A seventh argues that the analogy between social and natural science is erroneous. An eighth believes that the social sciences are not so much in need of new research techniques as of convictions based upon principles. A ninth says that the quest for methodological purism and its subsequent 'credo of relevance' are outdated and that there is need to resurrect normative political theory. And a tenth prefers to locate the durable dimensions of political theory in the analysis of propositions and concepts.

The endless fascinations to be found in political theory add to this confusion. Plato's fascination is the 'philosopher king'. Aristotle's ideal is the 'best practicable state'. Hobbes upholds undiluted sovereignty. Locke satisfies himself with a limited government based upon consent. Rousseau's noble savage ends up in general will and popular sovereignty. And the Marxists' ultimate aim is a stateless and classless society. Despite its hoary antiquity, political theory has rarely been able to evaluate Aristotle's 'political animal', the mythical 'economic man' of the classical economists, the equally imaginary 'reasonable and prudent man' of the lawyers, the 'natural man' of the contractualists, the 'alienated man' of the Marxian school, or the 'disenchanted man' of the technological age. It seems that political theory has been used like a blank cheque all along. It has become encrusted with all sorts of ideals, ideologies, propositions, concepts, models and operational theories. It not only encompasses an extremely broad spectrum of the information, concepts and doctrines and terminologies of every age, but also includes histories of political thought, methodologies, perception of institutions and the formulation of new categories. There always have been, are now and, probably, ever will be a number of opposed theoretical systems in political theory, each one claiming that it makes more sense than the others, and often terminating in quibbles, acrid discussions or erudite generalities. It is full of half-assimilated or heavily cultivated ideologies and sonorous or seductive phrases, and few realize the exact realities beneath the divergent viewpoints; the potential value of these depends on the user and how he uses them. It is difficult to frame a coherent pattern beneath the panoply of complex varieties and riddles found in political theory.

Moreover, the present age is one of crisis and revolution—in economics, in politics, in the social order and in the mind of the individual. Traditional and 'given' things are rejected as outmoded and irrelevant to the needs of the time. It is sad to record that traditional values, morals, beliefs, rules and methods are being looked upon with a wry eye. As such, ours has become an unphilosophical age, where the ideas and ideals formulated by long dead writers have been vastly neglected. One is dismayed to see that in contemporary theory, nothing comparable to stoicism has appeared as the intellectual and moral cement of a new society and polity. Mankind is still in a dissolving mood. Man has been uprooted today, the foundations of life are quaking beneath his feet, and he regards himself as dragged along in the wake of events which, when in a more sanguine mood, he had hoped to guide. There is in the climate of the modern world 'a sense of impending disaster, a rootlessness of the person, a pervasive tenseness which points to certainties dissolved and emotional centres displaced'. The uneasiness that exists today, or what Lewis Mumford calls 'the invisible breakdown in our civilization', the 'erosion of values, the dissipation of human purposes, the denial of any distinction between good or bad, right or wrong, the reversion to sub-human levels of conduct'[10], are, to a great extent, due to the fact that we are not living up to our moral capacity; we have been starving our purposes, developing our appetites, turning our hopes towards sublunary things, 'instead of the big ideas on which our lives and freedom depend'. The melancholy truth about the course of world history is that we are well along 'the road to disintegration' because of 'deterioration of personal, political and social morals'. If we wish to avert the decay and doom of our civilization, what is needed is a reemphasis on the study of the wondrous world of ideals in its quintessence. A philosophically illuminated political theory, in conjunction with other disciplines, could in the opinion of the author, 'play a central role in personal integration and social reconstruction and stability', for 'any improvement in practice will issue indirectly from it'. Only a political theory worthy in thought could be even more useful in action. As has been well observed by John Robinson, 'the task of the generation now in rebellion is to reassert the authority of morality over technology' and political theory alone can help to see both how necessary and how difficult that task is going to be. Of course, there are some who urge that 'political theory must once again be viewed as that form of knowledge which deals with what is general and integrative to man, a life of common involvements'. And some would argue that the 'value theory' is in shambles today. One student of contemporary political thought sums up the situation by remarking that to attempt the justification of ultimates leads 'to a bottomless morass'. The tragedy is that we have thrown overboard the sweet and honeyed lore of philosophy and values and are trying to implant in its place a lurid technical jargon, which is at its best a pale and ghastly substitute. Devoid of the lush fount of traditional philosophy, political theory today is enmeshed in a jungle of statistics, quantification and methodologies. It has lost its former gloss, the traditional greats are considered 'rascals' and a new shine or lustre in intellectual style is rarely visible. Neo-phrases and neo-idioms have been constructed with such great rapidity that they seem lifeless. The condition of modern political theory is like a bird attempting to fly, though its wings are broken. The craze for professional and specialized political theory relevant to society has been pushed to such an extreme degree that political theory has lost its 'conscience'. In its fondness for detachment and ethical neutrality, it has become inhuman and political passion has been lost in slumber. It has become a 'captive' of methodologies and techniques, and the great slogan that 'substance must precede technique' seems to be faltering. As such, an unprecedented identity crisis is sweeping over political theory and its vistas and mapping paths are shrouded in a tangle of confusion. This identity crisis has shaped considerably the intellectual styles in political theory.

Notes

1. Charles Vereker. 1964. *The Development of Political Theory* (London: Hutchinson University Library) p. 9.
2. William C. Baum. 1970. 'Political Theory', in *Political Science: The Discipline and its Dimensions*, (ed.) Stephen L. Wasby (Kolkata, Scientific Book Agency) p. 277.
3. C.E.M. Joad. 1973. *Introduction to Modern Political Theory* (Mumbai, Oxford University Press) p. 7.
4. David Easton. 1953. *The Political System* (New York, Knopf) p. 129.
5. Harold Lasswell. 1936. *Politics: Who Gets What, When and How* (New York, McGraw Hill) p. 2.

6. V.V. Thursby (ed.) 1969. *Contemporary Political Thought,* (New York, Holt, Rinehart and Winston) p. 27.
7. Bertrand de Jouvenel. 1963. *The Pure Theory of Politics* (Cambridge, Mass., Cambridge University Press) p. 30.
8. George Catlin. 1950. *A History of Political Philosophers* (London, George Allen and Unwin Ltd) p. 3.
9. Arnold Brecht. 1965. *Political Theory: The Foundations of Twentieth-Century Political Thought* (Mumbai, The Times of India Press) p. 10.
10. *The Conduct of Life*. 1951. (New York, Harcourt Brace) p. 148.

2

The Normative Style of Thinking

Political theory, today, is in a state of dilemma. This dilemma is further heightened by an incessant conflict between tradition and modernity. What was once at the centre of political theory has been pushed to the periphery, and what stood at the periphery has been thrust at the centre! The credo of the value-fact dichotomy and the unsatiated quest for factual knowledge, if it is knowledge at all, have blurred the vision of many contemporary theorists, who are not sure about the exact nature of their subject matter or their object world. Nor are they unanimous about their methodologies and techniques of research. Even if the path of an object world is clear, a theorist trained in the school of ethical neutrality would prefer to reach his destination through narrow lanes and side paths, demonstrating his fondness for data and quantification. This behavioural onslaught against political theory has created a predicament from which even the post-behaviouralists find it difficult to escape. In fact, so many intellectual styles, theories, models and generalizations have been cultivated about the field of political theory over a span of more than two thousand years that it is difficult even for a skilful surgeon to delineate its threads. The styles of rationalism and radical rationalism, the doctrines of natural law and natural rights, the ideals of utopia and organic community, the emergence of neo-Platonic and neo-Aristotelian visions, the streams of possessive individualism and scientific materialism, the thoughts of conservatism and anti-ideology, the intestinal faiths and cerebral theories, the Marxist and neo-Marxist styles, the positivists, neo-positivists and the critical-dialectical ideas, the growth of paradigms and analytical theories, and the endless debate over value-fact dichotomy, followed by a plea to reintegrate philosophy with science, wash over the domain of political theory in such a manner that it is well nigh impossible to count the waves. From classical times till today, so many intellectual styles have appeared and vanished, or reappeared and been modified, that one cannot safely locate all the parameters in political theory. Nevertheless, for the sake of convenience, one can at least point out the seminal styles in political theory. Broadly speaking, these are the normative, behavioural and post-behavioural styles. An analysis of each shall be attempted here.

The normative style in political theory is the oldest one. It rests on metaphysical, epistemological and ontological premises and is synonymous with thoughts, conjectures and ideas. It is also an appeal to an immanent or transcendental spirit, reason, truth or natural law. It serves to challenge the existing reality organizing principles. It views political theory in the framework of thought, speculation, ideas and philosophy. Its grand tradition extends through Plato, Aristotle, Rousseau, Hegel, Marx or even Laski. It includes political concepts almost totally oriented to the political community as an abstraction, towards legal authority and the institutions exercising it, and towards the proper relationship between the political order and the good life. It has an abiding interest in ethical and normative judgements. It is dominated by philosophy and the thinkers have often concentrated on 'ideal models' rather than 'process models'. It takes into consideration the questions of 'prescription and evaluation', focusing attention on the problem of 'what ought to be' rather than 'what actually happens'. Who should rule and why? What are the ends of the state and government? How is the moral development of an individual possible without hindering the evolution of the community? What are the proper means towards these ends? What is the best form of government? These questions dominate the style of normative theory, in which 'the analysis of the moral rather than of the strictly empirical world has stood at the peak of the theory's hierarchy of priorities'.

The normative style of political theory is closely related to philosophy, history, sociology, economics and allied subjects, and no need was felt to recognize politics as an 'autonomous subject of inquiry'. Political theory has been approached as an intellectual activity whereby the student could learn how he should go about exploring the knowable consequences and, through them, the ultimate premises of his own moral outlook. Political theory has been coated in a 'moral frame of reference' because politics is regarded here as a practice, a felicitous union of history and philosophy. Politics, the practitioners of this theory argue, is an art—a performing art and also a creative art. That is why, Plato once compared the politician to a flute player. Since politics is the highest form of art, its theory is bound to be value-laden. Only value-laden political knowledge can carry humanity forward out of the darkness of superstition, poverty and servility into a universal democratic civilization of liberty, equality and fraternity, where the laws are founded on reason and freedom. The normative style is in part an argument about values between men who agree about some values, but disagree about others. The dialogue is unending because there is no perfect knowledge of justice, and every man has to subscribe to his own order of axiological preference. Political theory is also an argument about the future consequences of proposed lines of action. As such, the normative style is mainly concerned with what 'ought to be done'—its task is to pass moral judgements. And political theory stands in close collaboration with ethics, for 'politics is but ethics writ large'.[1] Once we discuss politics, we are discussing right and wrong. And a discussion about right and wrong, properly treated, can be 'the most exciting thing in human experience'. The normative style, as such, is based on the real values of social life. Otherwise, its exponents argue that political theory is bound to be 'an abstract and a barren subject', useful only for professors who live by taking in each other's ideas and destroying them in the wash. It would now be desirable to take a look at the main paradigms that have pervaded the normative style.

The first style in normative theory can be called the noumenalist way of thinking. It 'equates the 'best' or 'rational' political order with a divinely ordained set of values (that is, ends and goals) and rules of behaviour which are understood as having the fullest or most perfect reality'.[2] The noumenalists can be divided into two groups—'transcendentalists' and 'immanentists'. Plato and Kant are examples of transcendentalists in a broad manner. They view the good order as wholly transcending the world of sense, the empirical world, incapable of any complete or permanent embodiment in a historical polity. Aristotle and Hegel are examples of immanentists. They find the rational order immanent in the world of sense as a potentiality and as a causal principle, giving form and meaning, and furnishing a principle of growth and development to empirical things. It is possible, as they see it, for a historical polity to grow into perfection. The noumenalist style, in general, holds that the good order is known by an intuitive faculty, or 'the ideological reason'—a useful phrase coined by Carl J. Friedrich.[3] The perfect order, according to some noumenalists like St Augustine and St Thomas Aquinas, can be grasped by faith and superior faculty, inspired by divine grace. The noumenalists do not agree, however, on the extent to which empirical men are perfectible, or capable of living the best life in the here and now. They also differ on the question of how we determine what our obligations are under less than ideal circumstances.

The second style in the normative mode of thinking is the naturalist theory, or naturalism. It is an assumption that reality, at least as far as we can know it, consists only of phenomena (for example, the theory of Hobbes). Reality is coextensive with the empirical world in this view. No intelligible essences or other forms of non-empirical reality lie beyond or behind this world to lend it being or significance. We order this phenomenal world with names which we ourselves create and which stand only for the appearances manifest to us through sense experience and introspection. The most striking thing about the world of experiences is its dynamic character. The images are in constant motion, ever changing from one into another. To understand it as an order, we impute causality to the relationships of the images, one to another. This theoretical construction, argue the naturalists, is more important as an instrument of prediction and control than as a means of understanding because they regard the world as essentially unintelligible. In naturalism, reason enters as an instrumentality. It supplies an efficient means for the fulfilment of the demands of passion, and it orders and balances the passions in such a way as to prevent their mutual frustration. Naturalism is a search for rational polity, based on the 'precepts of reason'; as such, it is the opposite of the noumenalist style.

The third style in normative theory is a blending of the two—the noumenalists and the naturalists. The theorists in this camp have been categorized as 'metaphysical bridge builders'. Aristotle is such a bridge builder. His treatise on metaphysics and the first three and last two books on *Politics* seem to place him squarely in the noumenalist camp. But his book on psychology, *De Anima,* and the central three books of *Politics* are strongly naturalistic in flavour. Bridge builders are also found among the naturalists. They can be grouped as pure naturalists, modified naturalists and teleo-naturalists. The pure naturalists are largely hedonists and individualists in their psychology, that is, in their reading of the pattern of passionate desires. The modified naturalists, by contrast, find sympathetic, benevolent and altruistic motives operating as a part of the fundamental, given order of human values. The teleo-naturalists even distinguish between higher and lower values and think it important to train men to give more regard than they do now to the higher ideals. Often, there are differences in these styles because these are concerned with various views of the good, the real, the knowable and the conception of the rational order.

The fourth style in normative theory is the conception of the entire political process in terms of 'virtue' and 'freedom'. The theories of 'virtue' enshrine the view that the stability of political systems, as well as their perfect fulfilment of purpose, depend on the moral character of both rulers and citizens. Plato is the supreme example of this. Even for Machiavelli, the viability of a political system requires moral integrity. In the paradigm of 'freedom', stability is assessed in terms of the degree to which citizens are secure in their freedom, whether this is the freedom of Hobbesian or Lockean property owners, the freedom conceived of as moral independence, as embodied in Rousseau's 'general will', the naturalistic interpretation of it wholly in terms of external liberty to act without restraint, the noumenalists' stress on moral freedom, or Hegel's absolute idea of seeking self-realization in freedom. Thus, 'freedom' becomes a conception of 'virtue', or goodness, in such theories.

The fifth style in normative theory is the theocratic paradigm. It is a combination of the mythic (magic and religion) and rationalistic styles. It upholds that from God came revelation, from revelation, reason, and from reason, natural law. From natural laws came practical ones such as those governing property, inheritance, military service and other obligations. Such practical injunctions and regulations, called positive law, are made by people and they indicate what is to be done and how. A true law is 'supreme reason consonant with nature, diffused among men, constant, eternal'. So, the theocratic paradigm consists of a mixture of natural law derived from the Greeks and Romans; revelations derived from the Christian belief system; positive law, which governs practical consequences; and grace, which represents the attainable purpose. To live in a state of grace, the ruled must be governed by positive laws, which alone can ensure proper conduct, devoutness, devotion, piety and work. The rulers establish positive law on the basis of reason and natural law and try to attain a good society or the city of God. In short, the theocratic paradigm insists that the 'true self of man' is not his 'flesh or bones or sinews, but the faculty which uses them', or reason. It is a 'jannock plea for pristine civic virtues', in the absence of which a state becomes 'highway robbery on a large scale'.

The sixth style in normative theory, contrary to the theocratic paradigm, is the tradition of enlightenment, which began in the sixteenth century. It lays emphasis on human beings rather than on God. It advocates that the ruler is a representative of the people with a constitutionally defined or limited sphere of power. It upholds that the political community consists not of private rights of all individuals, but of the rights of a representative assembly. It has secularized the notions of the rights of citizens and constitutional limits on the power of rulers and developed a rich corpus of contract theories. The contract theories have been the critical generative idea of modern constitutionalism.

The seventh style of normative theory is the radical paradigm. This is based on the Marxian premise that 'philosophers all along have interpreted the world, the point, however, is to change it'. It says that history is not a conflict between spirit and matter, it is not the unfolding of the spirit of the 'absolute'—it is 'nothing else than the activity of man pursuing his own aims'. Its most powerful exponent was Karl Marx, who sought to make radicalism into less of a vision and more of a science of socialism by applying a specific interpretation of history. Its emphasis is on how to promote new forms of politics. It has been a search for new generative ideas—in fact, a fusion of science and humanism. As a philosophy, it is a coherent whole. It is massive because revolutionary action is built upon the class war theory; the class war theory upon the economic theory of surplus value; this economic theory upon the economic interpretation of history; this interpretation upon the Marxo-Hegelian logic or dialectic; and this upon a materialistic metaphysic. This rational core of social philosophy has been presented with razor sharp conviction in Marxism. It is a system of ultimate ends and a guide to those ends, which implies a plan of salvation. It promises paradise on this side of the grave, and to millions of human hearts, it meant a new ray of light and a new meaning of life. It filled the emptiness of Marx's age and offered both the force of religious conviction and the certainty of apparently scientific proof. It was not only a revolutionary call to the working class, but equally, an assurance of its ultimate victory. Its theory of historical materialism and economic analysis, taken together, can fairly claim to be the greatest and most compelling statement of scientific socialism ever made. It is a philosophy of history, a theory of social development, a tactic, and an economic theory. It is equally a faith, a vision, a prophecy and a wish. It seems to offer a key for the unlocking of history. It marks a revolt against the past and gives to the individual the thrill of new adventure. Its powerful message awoke a responsive chord in the hearts of many men, and its exponent can be sure of his place in any collection of the world's great masters of political thought.

The eighth feature of the normative style is the concept of historicism as expounded by W.A. Dunning[4], C.H. Mcllwain[5] and G.H. Sabine[6]. Political theory, for Dunning, was a historical account of the conditions and consequences of political ideas. He held that the only path of approach to an accurate apprehension of political philosophy was through political history. He rejected the value of dealing with moral problems even in a purely historical context. He stuck to the belief that 'political theory is essentially historical research into views that derive from observation of political facts and practices, especially as they are related to the legal form of political life'. He virtually converted political theory into the history of factual ideas and theories. Another variation of historicism can be seen in the writings of Mcllwain. Where Dunning turned to history because he saw political ideas as a possible influence on the course of events, Mcllwain adopted historical research because, for him, a political idea was an effect, rather than an influential interacting part of social activity. A political theory, for Mcllwain, "is normally a rationalization, not a determinant or influential condition of action. Ideas are epiphenomena, the mere froth on the ocean, as it were, that has little effect on the movement of the waves. They justify behaviour, but are scarcely instrumental in influencing political activity." In spite of Mcllwain's reduction of political theory to the study of an aspect of history, there was embedded in his approach to the history of theory a respect for moral views that saved them from the utter eclipse they had suffered in Dunning's work. For Mcllwain, moral justifications appeared primary. In the opening comment of his work, Mcllwain has quoted with approval Rousseau's dictum: "Man is born free and everywhere he is in chains ... what can make it legitimate?" With this moral question from Rousseau, he set as his task the history 'of men's reflections about the moral basis of political obligation'.

A third type of historicism is represented by G.H. Sabine. Sabine falls into a separate category from that of Dunning or of Mcllwain. He combines elements from the approaches of both. He agrees with the former that the examination of political thought merits attention because it is an aspect of the political process that interacts with and influences social action. And he maintains with the latter the necessity of describing and analysing the moral judgements in each theory. Through this blend, he lays the basis for a serious inquiry into the values of various thinkers. For Sabine, moral judgements need not be viewed as mere rationalizations of activity; rather, they may be influential factors in history. As a subject matter, they are not inferior to factual proposition, as Dunning insisted by implication. As such, Sabine points out, every political theory can be examined from two points of view—as a social philosophy and as an ideology—and it contains two kinds of propositions—factual and moral.

The ninth feature of the normative style is the paradigm of institutionalism.[7] It upholds that the liberation political theories that have emerged from history as moral objectives are to be established in practice. It says that politics is an open conflict and is converted to competition, which is made peaceful by means of the instruments of representative government. Its problem is to find out what instrumentalities work best to realize the ideals of political philosophy. It gives special meaning to valuable instrumentalities, specific boundaries created by the constitution, transmission belts of public power, non-specific institutions and the connecting links. Its research is mainly formal and descriptive, its emphasis is on legal constitutional structures, and it takes human nature as constant. It lays stress on accumulation of facts, which are self-explanatory, and prefers to say that facts and values cannot be wholly separated. It puts reliance on documents (rules, laws, constitutions) and uncontrolled observations. It is reformist in orientation and its concern is for practical reforms, that is, ways to check power and stress on realizing democracy and constitutional government. Its primary problem is to maximize the concept of freedom with order. It aims to prevent a stalemate society and to promote an equilibrium society. It focuses more on appropriate legislation, reform of law, that is, on means rather than ends. This is the institutional 'how' of governing, which diluted the understanding of 'why'. As such, behaviouralism, while it did not fill the philosophical vacuum left by institutionalism, sought to examine the 'why' of politics by examining individual action.

The last feature of the normative style can be labelled as primitive empiricism.[8] Its research is more concerned with the political phenomenon. It uses empirical methods at the expense of intuition, argumentation and related methods. Its concern for political events leads to a regard for the dynamic elements of politics as well as the institutional framework. It is not as systematic or objective in procedure as are more recent examples of empiricism. Its rigour of observation and analysis is minimal, though its conclusions are in many cases extraordinarily accurate. For example, an analysis of political and social reality in several South American societies was undertaken by James Bryce early in the twentieth century. Bryce's conclusions were extremely accurate and were drawn from a sound empirical basis, but his methods for data collection and analysis were not always rigorous. In comparison, studies of contemporary political and social reality, such as those by Gabriel A. Almond and Sidney Verba[9], also have an empirical basis, but their data gathering methods are more rigorous.

The normative style as a whole has been put to severe stress by recent behaviouralist writers. They have practically rebelled against its major premises by using moving words, such as sloppy and imprecise, literary and selective, abstract and unsystematic, visionary and value-laden, idealistic and speculative, metaphysical and transcendental, impressionistic and subjective, and old fashioned and even primitive. The behaviouralists have styled the normative thinkers as 'idle speculators about human nature, navel-gazers and essayists'. They have been more worried about the language of the normative theory, which is, according to them, no more than a mere 'romance', or full of loose, literary, unrigorous and metaphorical style, and even dogmatic eloquence, but nothing more. They claim that it has lost its respectability because of wide and total disagreements. One writer describes this lack of agreement as the 'skeleton rattling in the philosophical cupboard'. Another writer seems to have in mind a basic redirection of philosophical tradition. He contends, "Reality ... has invalidated the historical relevance of philosophy." He sees 'pure' philosophy today as 'reduced to the order of an intellectual exercise'. One should not forget that though the powers of the normative style have been shaken, all is not lost. Although it may not be fully adequate, it is nevertheless indispensable for giving meaning to life. Its power of logical coherence, insightfulness and the moral desirability of its conclusions encourage a disciplined form of speculation, synthesis and even creative insight. It supplements scientific approach through both criticism and synthesis. Philosophy, one must never forget, is 'the criticism and the completion of science' because it is a rational and theoretical inquiry. Even the disagreement within the realm of philosophy is an element of strength because any sure method or procedure or agreed way of testing hypotheses would kill philosophy. Philosophy is the fissiparous mother of all sciences. This is no weakness, it is its potentiality.

Further, the normative style arouses politico-philosophical consciousness, or what Karl Jaspers characterizes as 'rational thought'. Let us not forget that something above politics must guide political institutions, legislations and designs if they are to endure. This 'supra-political' element is manifested in normative theory alone. The normative style can sharpen and strop our wits, clarify and redefine our thinking, and help reach coherent definitions and sounder moral appraisals. It encourages critical theory filled with curiosity, gives colour to human adventure and safeguards human living from the 'sterilized positivist utopia' of the behaviouralists. It alone is capable of ensuring continuity through time and change and is to human life what humus is to the planet. It is based on a critical revision, ever going on, of tradition in the light of current experience. It deals with the appraisals of social ends, where it has been touched up to luminousness and self-consciousness in the greatest reflective minds of each epoch. It studies history, not from the angle of heaped up granules of facts, but from that of the evaluating intelligence. It views the drama in each age through the eyes of the greatest minds of that time. It has been 'the dear delight' of Plato, in fact the front trench in the siege of truth. It has been the 'pleasure' of Will Durant, who could witness 'a lure even in the mirages of metaphysics'. It has been Leonardo's 'joy of understanding' and the 'highest music' for Pythagoras. Its powerful defence is reflected in the writings of Oscar Wilde, who says: "A map of the world that does not include Utopia is not worth even glancing at, for it leaves out the one country at which Humanity is always landing. And when Humanity lands there, it looks out, and seeing a better country, sets sail. Progress is the realization of Utopias." The realization of the concept of 'progress', to a great extent, depends upon the adoption of the normative style, which is 'an indispensable key' and an 'equally valuable guide'. The normative theory is 'the queen of theories', it is 'an adventure in ideas, and a romance of ideas'. In its absence, politics degenerates rapidly into purposeless motions and transactions, stagnation creeps into society, and man becomes a mere 'vocal beast'. If we wish to live well and 'avoid drifting aimlessly with the changing winds', we have to understand the 'whither' and the 'why'. Only those whose answers are logical and rational can escape 'joining Don Quixote in tilting at windmills'. In sum, normative activity opens our existence to new experiences and new styles of life by creating plausible futures. Through its method of merciless and devastating interrogation, it carries human beings through lush valleys of experience, across deserts of dogma, into deep forests of uncertainty, over perilous heights of theory, through raging torrents of controversy, striving ever to gain the elusive goal of perfect knowledge. To the thrill of intellectual exploration, it adds the thrill of the search for the ideal by a ruthless process of comparison and criticism. It is the idea that withstands every test of knowledge, every test of speculation, every test of logic, and emerges untarnished from this acid bath.

The normative style of thinking is value-laden, for it believes in the dictum of Kant that 'no political theory can ever advance a step further without first paying homage to the principles of morals and ethics'. Its value-laden element is not a point of weakness, as the behaviouralists argue; rather, it is a seminal current of vital importance. It fills theory with curiosity, gives colour to human adventure, sharpens and strops human wit, and helps mankind reach more coherent definitions and sounder moral appraisals. It is necessary for the 'emancipation of the mind' and in understanding political conflicts and power contests. It brings humanity in contact with the abundance of objects, where alone greatest happiness is possible. It is the essential intellectual weapon for any meaningful knowledge and academic dialogue of political phenomena. It provides leverage to significant social movements and revolutions by loading the contents of political theory with appraisals of social ends and social action. It reflects a critical revision, ever going on, of tradition in the light of current experience. It studies the history of ideas, not from the angle of heaped up granules of fact, but from that of the evaluating intelligence. It provides a norm and a canon with which to judge new theories. It can lead us towards political betterment and the dawn of a new free society. It is a leisured feast of reason and helps to make us aware of the mission of man. It, no doubt, differs from one thinker to another, and in this difference alone lies the essence of education, as Diderot said, in the stirring of doubt and wonder. It would, therefore, be futile to build political theories in the absence of normative value premises. Its canons are even necessary for making scientific observations of facts and in analysing their causal interrelationships; from this viewpoint, a disinterested political theory is 'pure nonsense'. Its evasion would make a political theorist some sort of 'minotaur'—'a monster with a human body and the head of a bull, or the man–beast, or the cleft creature'. As such, political science is 'not so much in need of new research techniques as of convictions based upon principles'. A political theory that 'is not committed to the search for freedom and justice has already signed its death warrant'. A political theory without normative values would, therefore, be myopic and even suicidal for society as a whole. The normative style alone can help in providing political theory with 'the greatest clarity and imaginative beauty'. It aims at the development of 'the health, harmony, beauty, excellence' of the whole man. It tries to pulverize the evils facing mankind with its ideal that philosophy must rule the state.[10] It gives recommendations on how men should conduct politics,[11] and above all, it is a quest for a 'rationally planned society',[12] where the policies of the concrete political world can go out 'to kill the dragons of stupidity and greed'.

The normative way of thinking can never be totally uprooted from political theory, whatever may be the intensity of the blasts by its enemies, especially the behaviouralists. The behaviouralists have often proclaimed that political theory is dead, or sadly diminished in importance, or in a stage of 'demise', 'decline' or decay. This so-called decline is attributed to several factors. Its main causes of decline, according to David Easton, are historicism, moral relativism, hyperfactualism, confusion over the use of the terms, 'science' and 'theory', and its failure to develop a new synthesis. Its decay, says Alfred Cobban, is due to its internal conditions and the external environment of the State. Its main cause of decline, argues S.M. Lipset, is the triumph of the democratic social revolution in the West. Its other causes of decline, as often advocated by the behaviouralists, are the ideological reductionism of Tracy, Comte and Marx, logical positivism, linguistic philosophy and neo-positivism. This so-called 'decline' of political theory is rather unreal, for despite its imperfections, normative theory is not dead—it is up again. Dante Germino has made a fascinating plea regarding the ascendency of the normative theory; he argues that metaphysics and ontology are legitimate and indeed central fields of inquiry. Ideological messianism, beliefs and programmes of reform are the dominant forces in the contemporary age and this itself speaks of the relevance of political philosophy.

Even in the writings of other contemporary political theorists, there is a strong tendency towards the revival of political theory. The Italian thinker, Benedetto Croce, and the French philosopher, Henri Bergson, have admirably offered intellectual resistance to the ideological reductionism of Tracy, Comte and Marx. There are other thinkers—such as Julien Benda, Max Schaler, Nicolai Hartmann and A.N. Whitehead—who have cooperated in the venture of the revival of traditional theory. Added to this are exponents such as Michael Oakeshott, Hannah Arendt, Bertrand de Jouvenel, Leo Strauss and Eric Voegelin, who refuse to oblige the proponents of the demise of political theory thesis. Further, there are notable contributions to the examination of political concepts. The most significant contemporary contributions in this regard are: Rawl's concept of 'justice', Hart's concept of 'law', Cranston's new analysis of 'freedom',

Hanna Pitkin's concept of 'representation', Plamenatz's concept of 'consent, freedom and political obligation', Patridge's concept of 'consent and consensus', Martin Albrow's concept of 'bureaucracy', and Ioan Davies' analysis of the concept of 'social mobility and political change'. This revival of political theory does not mean the acceptance of the normative principles in toto, or the clear cut rejection of the scientific way of inquiry in analysing political issues. It means the rejection of the claims of methodological superiority and pure metaphysics. It is an attempt to combine the realms of fact finding, systematic knowledge and theory building on the one hand, and the sphere of social policy, political problems and ideological issues on the other. It is in this sense that the normative style has been restored in political theory. This 'rebirth' is indeed 'a truly creative flowering' and the 'renaissance of political theory in the grand manner'. As such, 'like the proverbial phoenix, political theory is today rising from the ashes of its own destruction, and rather than schedule its funeral, we should instead be rejoicingly commemorating its rebirth'.[13] Political theory, therefore, is being increasingly viewed today 'as that form of knowledge which deals with what is general and integrative to man, a life of common involvement'.[14] Enclosed in nothing but an empirical framework, political theory is a contradiction in terms and a monstrosity. In the absence of a philosophic framework, theory is 'bound to be without direction and barren of meaning'.

Notes

1. Ivor Brown. 1929 *English Political Theory* (London, Methuen) p. 2.
2. William T. Bluhm. 1911. *Theories of the Political System* (New Delhi, Prentice-Hall of India Pvt. Ltd) p. 10.
3. *Inevitable Peace*. 1948. (Cambridge, Mass., Harvard University Press) p. 129.
4. *A History of Political Theories*.1902. (New York, Macmillan).
5. *The Growth of Political Thought in the West.* 1932. (New York, Macmillan).
6. *A History of Political Theory*. 1937. (New York, Henry Holt).
7. Louis D. Hayes and Ronald D. Hedlund (eds). 1970. *The Conduct of Political Inquiry: Behavioural Political Analysis.* (Englewood Cliffs, N.J., Prentice-Hall, Inc.) p. 5.
8. Ibid. p. 5.
9. *The Civic Culture.* 1963. (Princeton, N.J., Princeton University Press).
10. R.L. Nettleship. 1961. *Lectures on the Republic of Plato* (London, Macmillan) p. 12.
11. Thomas Landon Thorson. 1962. *The Logic of Democracy* (New York, Holt, Rinehart and Winston, Inc.) pp. 68–9.
12. G.C. Field. 1963. *Political Theory* (London, Methuen) p. 4.
13. Dante Germino. 1963. 'The Revival of Political Theory', in *The Journal of Politics,* Vol. 25, August, pp. 437–60.
14. Sheldon S. Wolin. 1960. *Politics and Vision* (Boston, Mass., Little Brown and Co.) p. 434.

3

The Behavioural Mode of Political Analysis

The second intellectual style that rocked political theory, especially after the end of World War II, is the vigorous quest for scientific politics. This has been styled as the behavioural revolution in political science and is considered by its exponents to be the paramount development in the discipline's entire intellectual history. It is a frenzied, but bloodless, revolt against the normative style of thinking and it set the tone for political research for some two decades or so. Its intellectual origins are complex. Its spiritual ancestor was the sceptical philosophy of David Hume. Its American forerunner was the pragmatic philosophy of William James (1842–1910), which emphasized empiricism, voluntarism, the actions of individuals, and the connection between consciousness and purpose. Such concerns were compatible with the Lockean principles of individualism, adding to them psychological variables that could be used to explain individual behaviour. Its exponents were aware of the shift Graham Wallas (1858–1932) made from an economic model of politics to a psychological one. Another of its forerunners was the philosophy of Charles S. Pierce (1839–1914), who invented the term, 'pragmatism'. And, perhaps, an even more important forerunner was John Dewey (1859–1952), who sought to construct a practical philosophy of truth based not on ideal principles, but on the observation of experience. Dewey's 'instrumentalism', in particular, saw truth as conceived and tested in experience, and linked philosophy to psychology; thus, with this emphasis, philosophy became 'scientific', or an observational pursuit. It was John B. Watson (1878–1958), a psychologist, who coined the term, 'behaviouralism', and considered learning to occur as a result of observations of the connections between stimuli and responses. It was this 'behavioural instrumentalism' that threw overboard the speculative mode, the rationalistic or logical deductive analysis of political philosophers. It saw philosophy and history fundamentally at odds with behavioural experimental methods. It was only interested in the philosophy of science as exemplified in the works of Alfred North Whitehead, Rudolf Carnap, Carl Hempel and Karl Popper. Its object was to supplant metaphysical perspectives, replacing probability with certainty, rationalism with measures of central tendency, and description with distributions and measures of dispersion. It was in favour of more rigorously developed empirical generalizations based on observation and, as such, it was historical and non-evolutionary. It preferred a natural science paradigm and was linked to Saint-Simon's doctrine of positivism, which emphasized scientific methods. Its powerful intellectual forerunners were the exponents of the Chicago School of behaviouralism. It also drew its inspiration from the Vienna Circle and the traditions represented by Poincare, Frege and Wittgenstein, who were interested in the link between experimentalism and scientific philosophy and sought to locate the principles of a unified science of human behaviour and to link politics to 'system theory'. It was this idea which was developed later on by David Easton, who offered a new scientific orientation called general systems analysis.

There were several factors that promoted the growth of behaviouralism. First, there was widespread dissatisfaction with the 'state of discipline'. This stemmed from several sources: the discovery that the talents and skills of political scientists were not highly valued by governmental personnel; the disconcerting realization by those who did spend some time in public service of the profound difference between the 'accepted wisdom' of the profession and the reality of the governmental process; the inability of traditional political theory to account for the rise of fascism, national socialism and communism, or to explain the continuance of these regimes in power; a growing sensitivity to and unhappiness with the basically descriptive nature of the discipline; and a knowledge of apparent advances in other social sciences and the mounting fear that political science was lagging behind its sister professions. Secondly, the post-war experiences with technical assistance, expanding state activity and economic aid programmes contributed to the sense of malaise. The various efforts to export US political and administrative knowhow forced upon American political scientists a painful awareness that much of their vaunted experience applied, if at all, only to the type of political and administrative problems encountered in Western, industrialized societies. This discovery provided a powerful impetus to the quest for cross-cultural and trans-national regularities, which has characterized one aspect of behavioural inquiry. Thirdly, the migration of European social scientists to the US during the 1930s and 1940s gave an impetus to the winds of change. These social scientists exposed their American hosts to the currents of thought (Max Weber, logical positivism, etc. from which behaviouralism was to borrow heavily. The fourth factor was the expanding use of public opinion polls and the refinement of survey techniques. And lastly, a good deal of behavioural research was made possible by funding agencies that were partial to behaviouralism.

The history of behaviouralism can be divided broadly into two parts: the first behavioural movement and the second behavioural revolution. The first or early phase of the behavioural movement—during the 1920s and the 1930s—had an empirical and quantitative thrust. This movement is best exemplified by Stuart Rice and Harold Gosnell, who urged the introduction of quantitative methods that were being used within related disciplines in the social sciences; though 'the notion of science' had also appeared in the writings of Charles Merriam, Catlin and Munro. It relied more on statistical tables and the methodological sophistication in analysing such data was at a low level. Its methods were merely adapted to enable a somewhat more precise description and analysis of the prevailing and enduring paradigms of political science. Its exponents were substantively oriented and urged a shift from the level of impressionistic description to the level of detailed factual description. It was amorphous in nature and 'the term served as a sort of umbrella, capacious enough to provide a temporary shelter for a heterogeneous group united only by dissatisfaction with traditional political science'.

The second phase, or the behavioural revolution, was a rather significant one. Its main exponents were David B. Truman, Gabriel Almond, Robert A. Dahl, David Easton, Heinz Eulau, Evron M. Kirkpatrick, Mulfred Q. Sibley and, most prominently, Harold Lasswell. It called attention to the need to formulate and to test propositions. It introduced a spate of theoretical schemes, research designs and pleas for theory building in the 1950s. It urged an end to the overly monographic character of political science. It encouraged theoretical innovations such as the systems approach, decision making theory and communications theory, and moved political theory towards an emphasis on empirical theory. It vastly developed analytical edifices and research techniques to test theory. It envisaged and encouraged quantitative advances, but only insofar as techniques were a means to theory building. It created a cluster of systematic case analyses, content analyses, surveys, experiments, aggregate statistical analyses and causal modelling. It was enthusiastic about adopting mathematical techniques and multivariate analyses. However, a kind of retrogression took place around the 1960s, when quantitative strategies advanced far beyond the theoretical equipment at hand and many theoretical innovative behaviouralists failed to keep abreast of the newer advances in research technology. As a result, its exponents became fragmented into parochial schools of thought and, occasionally, could even be seen to be in warring camps. One school of theoretical behaviouralism continued to spin webs of theory, unchecked by substantive findings. Another school, called positive behaviouralists, moved to brute or barefoot empiricism and their thinking with prevailing methods seemed unrelated to theory. A third category, the non-behaviouralists, having been attracted towards these orientations, found themselves gravitating toward one of the two choices, leaving the traditional category as a residual for non-quantitative, non-theoretical scholars. It is significant to note that the positivist and theoretical behaviouralists were remarkably isolated from each other in intellectual stimulation and rapport and could be seen in warring camps at professional conferences and seminars. It was viewed as a serious cleft between the two, for they did not have a common idiom—each retreated to esoteric havens called 'theory' and 'research'. It was only with the arrival of David Easton that the consequences of this new cleft were delineated from a normative perspective. He provided a new orientation called 'multimethodologism', or an attempt to combine theoretical sophistication and advanced research technology. He sought to propound a basic consensus, or the major tenets of behaviouralism. The articles of faith[1] and style of this consensus can be identified as under:

1. Political science is closer to biology than to physics or chemistry and, ultimately, it can become a science capable of prediction and explanation. As such, a political theorist should engage in an unrelenting search for regularities of political behaviour and for the variables associated with them. He should, therefore, eschew purely descriptive studies in favour of the rigorous, analytical treatment essential to the systematic development of political knowledge.
2. Political science should concern itself primarily, if not exclusively, with phenomena that can actually be observed, that is, with what is done or said. This behaviour may be that of individuals and/or of political aggregates.
3. Data should be quantified and findings should be based upon quantifiable data. Only quantification can make possible the discovery and precise statement of relationships and regularities.
4. Research should be theory oriented and theory directed. Ideally, inquiry should proceed from carefully developed theoretical formulations, which, in turn, yield 'operationalizable' hypotheses, that is, hypotheses that can be tested against empirical data. Since theory must take into account the nature, scope and variety of the phenomena under study, the behaviouralists speak of 'low level', 'middle level' and 'general theory'. The ultimate objective is the development of 'over-arching' generalizations, which accurately describe and interrelate political phenomenon in the same

fashion that Newton's laws once seemed to account for the physical world.

5. Political science should abjure, in favour of 'pure' research, both applied research aimed at providing solutions to specific, immediate social problems and melioratory programmatic ventures. These efforts produce little valid scientific knowledge and represent, instead, an essentially unproductive diversion of energy, resources and attention.
6. Political theorists should broadly abandon the prevailing 'great issues'. The contention that political science has no proper concern with moral or ethical questions as such has been one of the most bitterly argued aspects of behaviouralism.
7. Political scientists should be more interdisciplinary. Political behaviour is only one form of social behaviour and the discipline would profit tremendously by drawing on the skills, techniques and concepts of its sister social sciences. Some behaviouralists even deny whether political science constitutes a true discipline in itself or not.
8. Political science should become more self-conscious and critical about its methodology. Its practitioners should develop a greater familiarity with and make better use of such tools as multivariate analysis, sample surveys, mathematical models and simulation. They should make every effort to be aware of and to discount their own 'value' preferences in planning, executing and assessing their research undertakings.

This, then, is the behavioural style in political theory.

It is a bold attempt to state that the study of political science, like the other sciences, 'rests on facts'.[2] Its remarkable messages—'the root is man'; 'the goal is man'[3]—reflect a didactic approach to political behaviour and focus attention on the phenomenon of government in terms of the 'observed and the observable'. It even hopes that the revolution 'will assist in the rapidly evolving maturity of political science as a rigorous theoretical discipline with a core and theory more systematic and challenging than it has heretofore been'.[4] It calls for a greater interest in political reality, concerning itself primarily with the description and analysis of political behaviour, thus encouraging 'methodological meliorism' and welcoming the demise of the 'moral philosophy approach' as a golden opportunity for achieving the long awaited breakthrough to a new era of empirical political science. It accepts as admissible only such knowledge that is inductive, quantifiable, objectively verifiable and specific, while rejecting as unsubstantiated, subjective or even worthless and propositions that rest on any other foundation. It condemns methods that claim justification through wisdom, insight and intuition. It is not inclined towards common sense; it prefers the technical mastery of method for political theorists. It implies a type of training and, ultimately, a type of professional personality. It is 'nothing more than the application of precise scientific methods to the study of politics'. It states flatly that 'the discovery of truth is an object of specialized research'. It says that neither people, nor politicians, nor philosophers are equipped for the pursuit of the truths about society; only scientists who follow certain prescribed methods can penetrate the nature of social reality. It rejects political theory 'in the grand manner' because it 'can rarely, if ever, meet the rigorous criteria of truth'. It goes on to elucidate that these criteria are the same severe standards of evidence required of scientific work. It asserts that a political theory has to take the notion of testability seriously.

The behavioural revolution in political science has been able to cast a certain amount of influence on the development of political theory. It has made political science more self-conscious and self-critical. It upholds that the world of man and society might be most effectively made intelligible and perhaps controlled by the use of naturalistic categories and techniques.[5] It has brought about dramatic changes in vocabulary. It does not speak about the notions of checks and balances, state, sovereignty, dual federalism, natural consent, issues, state of nature, dialectical materialism, or the greatest good of the greatest number. It uses such exotic phrases as boundary maintenance, bargaining, cognitive dissonance, community power structure, conflict resolution, conceptual framework, cross-pressures, decision making, dysfunctionality, factor analysis, feedback, homeostasis, input–output, interaction, models, multiple regression, multivariate analysis, non-parametrics, pay-offs, transaction flow models, roles, simulation, systems analysis and, of course, political socialization. It has borrowed most of its concepts and terms from other disciplines. It has paid increased attention to research techniques and to analytic theory. It has made a massive import of theoretical approaches and analytical methods. It has made most of the departments of political science in the US heavily oriented toward methodology. It has left its mark on almost every specialization within the discipline and produced studies in the field of community politics, electoral behaviour, political socialization, political culture and public opinion. It turns its attention away from legal and constitutional arrangements to observe individual political action. This does not mean that research is restricted to the individual person as the theoretical focus of investigation. It includes a small group, an organization, a community, an elite group, a mass movement or even a national society for its inquiry and events. Its categories of analysis are structures, functions, processes, or their relations. It insists on knowing 'what is true' of public activity and, therefore, turns its attention to variables such as relationships, strategies of action, and the effects of variables such as size, number and saliency. As one model or style of approach in the long chain of political theory, it has shifted the balance of concern from prescription, ethical inquiry and action to description, explanation and verification. It holds that without the accumulation of reliable knowledge, the means for the achievement of goals would be so uncertain as to convert action into a futile exercise. Despite all this, behaviouralism is not the last word in political science. It has never been fully absorbed into the discipline. Its pure research has been consumed by a small fraction of political scientists. It has, to a considerable degree, led to the 'Americanization' of political science and is even regarded by many as 'a seventh subfield' of the discipline. It has been categorized as an analytically innovative movement and has prepared the way for an iconoclastic political science, urging and practising scientific canons of inquiry. Its ideal commitments have been technical proficiency in the search for reliable knowledge, the pursuit of basic understanding with its necessary divorce from practical concerns, and the exclusion of value specification as beyond the competence of science. It is these ideals that behavioural research has sought to import into the discipline of political science.

Whatever the impact of behaviouralism, it is fraught with severe debilities. Its excessive concern for verbal artifices in political inquiry has introduced intellectual barrenness and logical diffusiveness. Its indifference to values, or ethical neutrality, has trivialized political theory, leading to a monumental accumulation of data and a meagre crop of ideas.[6] Its failure to give new life and new direction to political science has been highlighted by McCoy and Playford, when they say that behaviouralists have 'concocted their own ivory tower out of jargon and scientism' and 'they are apolitical, having failed to address those genuinely significant problems' which concern us most. It has established methodology 'as the most relevant criteria for research' and thereby 'turn(ed) the students of politics into political eunuchs'.[7] Its craze for 'methodism' has impoverished education and restricted imagination. Its relentless efforts to produce 'processed voters'[8] have sacrificed political relevance on the altar of methodology. Its theorists have failed to match the creative work done in the field of political theory. Its writers can hardly equal the profundity of the works of Plato, Aristotle, Hobbes, Locke, Rousseau, Mill and Marx, or the loftiness of style that is visible in the works of E.F. Carritt, L.T. Hobhouse, T.P. Plamenatz, R.H. Tawney, A.D. Lindsay, E. Barker and H.J. Laski. Even in realistic imagination, its adherents stand nowhere in comparison to the likes of Morris Cohen, Reinhold Niebuhr, T.V. Smith,

Carl Becker, Thurmond Arnold, Adolf Berle, Sydney Hook and James Burnham. It has not been able to develop a political theory which can claim to be a major integrative process in all human societies.

Behaviouralism has invaded and rocked political science because of its tireless tirade against metaphysics and values. Its defenders have raised the question whether there is at all a place for prescriptive theory in the scientific study of politics. It has created a considerable noise against the adequacy and productiveness of classical theory, dismissing it 'as peripheral to the study of the real political world'. Its attempts to build up scientifically valid political theories, capable of explanation and prediction, appear, on close examination, to be superficial, half-baked and unscholarly. Its assertion that politics is an objectively ordered structure analogous to the order of nature, which can be successfully penetrated by the mathematized natural sciences, has led to fustian jargon and fluffy intellectual insights. Its basic presumptions that the political phenomenon can be studied rigorously, and precise generalizations, immutable regularities and uniform models formulated, have proved faulty and unsound in view of the dynamic buoyancy and malleable character of political processes, and in view of the fact that 'the extraordinary complexity of human behaviour cannot be systematically reduced'.[9] Its basic stand that precise scientific forecasts of every kind of political fact and event is possible is erroneous and impossible to realize. Its ideology has sadly neglected the wisdom of Proudhan's remark: "The fecundity of the unexpected far exceeds the statesman's prudence." Behaviouralism's measurements and quantification techniques and the polls and samples and games and models so much in vogue in contemporary political research may yield some information, but will seldom reach the core of the discipline. Its statistical exactitude and voting behaviour studies, where 'methodological purism' and amassed data act as a dead weight of intellectual lumber, is like the foam on the current of a river. Its preference for exact statistical answers over less exact, politically relevant answers has jeopardized political theory. It strives to define the technique first and the problem second, thereby driving a cleft into the heart of political studies. Its neologisms burst like roman candles in the sky and wars of epistemological legitimacy are fought incessantly. Its devotees are the devotees of rigour and nomological precepts and the low level and middle range theories they have propounded are sheer 'non-knowledge'. It has thrust human reason into any handy cubbyhole and maintained that observed behaviour, minus consciousness, can actually suffice for the governance of men. Its factual data of politics is never judged and appraised by moral criteria. It forgets that the actual and the ideal are dough and yeast, and it is in unison that they become a food fit for consumption. It neglects direction points or ultimate goals that are ideally conceivable. It never takes into consideration that politics is a search for ends as well as means, or that it is 'the art of the possible'. Its exponents, despite the time, energy and enormous sums of money consumed, have not been able to acquire scientific knowledge of voting behaviour or discover the real regularities underlying voting patterns. Trudging through tedious routes and data laden bypaths, it has at best been able to propound low level theories that are of negligible political interest. Its researchers, after collecting a heap of data, say: "Socioeconomic status is directly related to the final vote decision"; or, "The younger Catholics vote more Republicans"; or, "The higher one's sense of political efficacy, the higher the level of his participation in the election"; or, "The Harijans prefer the Congress"; or, "Caste is a factor to be reckoned with in the election"; or, "Despite the difficulties, the special privileges have been beneficial for the scheduled castes"; or, "If the economic status of the Harijan community is improved, their educational aspirations can be easily fulfilled"; or, "The district bureaucracy is slowly trying to modernize itself"; or, "Little boys like to play with little boys and little girls with little girls"; or, "If, in a given society, an aunt resided with or near the mother and assisted in giving care to the child, the latter would regard her as a mother, less so or not so than if the aunt lived at a distance"; and so on. What is the relevance of these low level statements, arrived at after spending huge sums of money? Are they meaningful? Are they of any political interest? The point is that behaviouralism has faltered badly in producing a single law of human behaviour comparable to the heights of Machiavelli and Hobbes. Its inability to distinguish the multiple causes behind even the simplest human behaviour has impaired the growth of a sound political theory. Its findings have often been of the ordinary dinner table variety—casual and desultory. It has not been able to produce a single grand theory; whatever fragmentary findings or low level theories it has produced are socially inconsequential. Its efforts to define its problems by facts, and not by social and political norms, have contributed to inaction because, in it, facts are merely holes in punch cards, and data without sinews and muscles is a mere skeleton. If behaviouralism becomes widespread, it would 'destroy' political theory as the philologists have destroyed literature, and historians, history.[10] It ought to be remembered that political theory 'cannot escape philosophic arguments about the nature of man, free will or determinism, rational and instinctive behaviour, the meaning of progress and of change, the quality of human life'.[11] Let behaviouralists remember that a writer is a political philosopher before he is a political scientist,[12] and political philosophy is more than mere intellectual gymnastics on political theory.

Behavioural ideology has introduced the worst kind of parochialism in political science. Its quest for a generalization of political science is necessarily useless; it is a naïve view methodologically. It has produced a false and dangerously misleading political theory—a theory denying that political society develops, or that it ever changes significantly, or that political developments can affect the basic regularities of political life. It introduces artificial controls, artificial isolation and, thereby, formulates generalizations based on the idea that where circumstances are similar, similar things will happen. Nothing is more dangerous in political science than this. Political experiments are not performed in a laboratory detached from the outside world and, in political history, real repetition is impossible, which means that one must expect that events of an intrinsically new character will emerge. Of what use are its models and theories, where nothing can repeat itself precisely and real novelty is always emerging? As such, its general laws seldom take into account the unique role of personalities and the complexity of political phenomena. Its attempts to prove that the subject matter of political science can be artificially simplified and immutable political uniformities arrived at, have proved hazardous. It seldom takes into consideration the full and complicated interaction between 'observer and observed', between subject and object. It even fails to take into account the peculiar complexity arising from the interconnection between predictions and predicted events. Its whole premise that political science can ultimately become a science capable of prediction and. explanation has tumbled down. Its quantitative and factual hunger are sweeping the social sciences to moral 'nihilism'. Its undivided mechanical and unthinking approach to the study of human behaviour is defective and culpable. It views human beings as an engineer would view materials for building bridges. It neglects the perspectives of political experience and looks at things from the viewpoint of 'scientific psychology' in the same manner as one would look at triangles, or fish in a glass chamber. It has abandoned politics for a kind of pseudo-psychology, or ersatz sociology. It cannot begin to open its dialogue without an extensive, technical vocabulary and tortured polemic. It has rendered prose tortuous and dull and impedes communication with logy arithmetic. Its fondness for semantic jugglery has shut the doors on the moral development and angelic excellence of man. It has dehumanized politics and belittled the stature and dignity of man. Its balderdash glossary of words aims to reduce man as a whole, in all his activities, to the level of a conditioned and behaving animal. It has virtually destroyed our grasp of political reality through positivist reduction. It makes no effort to cope with politics as part of the full range of human experience. Its technology attempts to transform man beyond recognition by pushing him into a computerized chamber. Its omission and ostracism of values and its crude clinical detachment have created a 'validity gap' in the domain of political theory. It seems that through the years, the behaviouralists have been playing blind man's buff. In their search for contentless technical fantasy, they have thrown away a crown for a servant's cap.

Behavioural political science 'looks for laws of human behaviour to be discovered by means of data supplied through certain techniques of research which are believed to guarantee the maximum of objectivity; therefore, it puts a premium on the study of things that occur frequently now in democratic societies; neither those in their graves nor those behind the curtains can respond to questionnaires or to interviews'. In its attempt to eschew values, it destroys the possibility of self-respect. It places a premium on observations that can be made with the greatest frequency 'and therefore by people of the meanest capacities', often culminating 'in observations made by people who are not intelligent about people who are not intelligent'. It is not diabolic—it has none of the attributes of fallen angels. Nor is it Machiavellian, for Machiavelli's teachings were graceful, subtle and colourful. Nor is it Neronian: 'One may say of it that it fiddles while Rome burns', but 'it does not know that it fiddles, and it does not know that Rome burns'.

Behavioural ideology is rooted in logical positivism and ends up creating a political theory, which (a) reduces itself to sociology—the study of groups, (b) is connected with dogmatic atheism, (c) seeks a more precise language and ends up more vague than ordinary language, (d) regards all values as equal, which they are not, (e) shows amazing disproportion between the apparent breadth of its goal (say, a general theory of social change) and the true pettiness of the research undertaken to achieve that goal, (f) shows indifference to the idea of goodness, (g) is unable to predict the outcome of the unprecedented conflict peculiar to our age, and (h) culminates frequently in 'formalistic' and 'vulgarian' observations. It has thus given birth to a theoretical Loch Ness monster in political science, for one can say with confidence what it is not, but it is difficult to say what it is. It is virtually an empty bottle into which one may presumably pour any kind of wine, new or old, as it is aromatic of science. Political theory, under its engineering, is no more than a specific corpus of accumulated knowledge, cultivated and added to by a special group of professional political scientists, the cardinal feature of which is a hybrid mixture of meaningless jargon and pretentious platitudes and truisms. It thus limits political theory to a mere bark or purr of dogs and cats and throws up witless theories, devoid of key intellectual problems and central moral values. The multiplication of behavioural models, like the population of monkeys in a rainforest or of insects under a paving stone, has encouraged sloppy thinking in political science and trivialized theory. In trying to refute the normative theory, behaviouralists are attempting to 'dissipate a fog by flinging hand-grenades into it'. Such a theory is inaccurate and incomplete for it dresses up political–social inquiries in pseudo-scientific clothes, a theme which has been brilliantly expounded by Stanislav Andreski in his concisely explosive work, *Social Sciences as Sorcery*.

Harold Lasswell, the greatest doyen ever born, has been the godfather for behavioural political scientists. Lasswell's models are informed by 'a thorough-going empiricist philosophy of the sciences', based on 'logical positivism, operationalism, instrumentalism'. The Lasswellian models are saturated with tables and graphs, data and techniques, and jargon and mathematical elaborations, so much so that political theory has been pushed into a foul nest of loathsome technical tapestry. Their cybernetic dialects and ratchet-like mechanisms have reduced political theory to vacuity, by taking out from humanity's aviary the noble value-laden bird. They are radically defective models because they lack radiant vision and ignore the economic man, political man and religious man. They make our minds like skeleton locks for which keys are not available. True, they possess low level theory, methodology and epistemology to support their findings. But alas, they have no better understanding of human beings than the bewildered savages of the jungle. They are nothing more than a mumbo jumbo of technical fantasy. They insist on computerizing human behaviour, and for them, the human being is like an engine: Push a button and the engine starts, press a pedal and the vehicle moves—that is the magic that the Lasswellian models have brought about in the realm of political studies. Their scientific–empirical framework and political technology, with their relentless insistence on specialization and expertise, have come full circle and been transformed into 'as closed a priesthood as any in history'. The reality which Lasswellian knowledge examines cannot be translated into either art or ritual in which the community can participate in and experience. The information and data of these models cannot be popularized as a form of vital experience. Such is the price that one has to pay in the aloofness of objective knowledge as assiduously developed by the Lasswellian style. The worst tragedy in the whole development of political theory is that things, events and human behaviour can be known only by the Lasswellian models. Man is best understood, say the Lasswellian models, when seen from the level of a rodent eager to learn the ins and outs of a maze. He can be conditioned to put up with almost anything the few wise designers of the maze have mapped out for him. This cult of Lasswellian quantification is a cynical view of man: It is a dog like, or even a rat like, view of man. A famous archaeologist once complained that the advent of photography had corrupted the young generation of scholars in the field. They no longer needed to draw what they saw. They simply shot a picture, but in the process of doing this, they forgot, or never learned in the first place, how to observe. Drawing with a pencil on white paper some glimpses deep down in a cave was hard schooling. It taught the young scholars how to see. Similarly, I am afraid, the arrival and pushing of the Lasswellian models in political science have corrupted young scientists and theorists. They are so proud of the presumed power of statistical tools, of measurement of attitudes, for instance, that they never learn how to observe significant phenomena in their field of study. They learn all about 'measuring' attitudes before they can tell one attitude from another by looking at a human being in social action.

Can Lasswellian theories lead us to excellence and social renewal?[13] The renewal of societies and of individuals depend in some measure on motivation, commitment, conviction, the values men live by, and the things that give meaning to their lives. The Lasswellian models falter badly on this criterion and they will eventually bring civilization to mouldering ruin. They are like a mad scientist, who, fingering the switches on his electronic computer, declared: "The individual is obsolete. We can survive only if society runs like a finely tuned machine. That requires suppression of individuality." As such, we must put a halt to the Lasswellian ghost or we shall lose the creative spark that renews both societies and men. Can we foster versatile, innovative and self-renewing men and women through the Lasswellian models? Are the Lasswellian models relevant for generating zest and generosity? Are they relevant to human beings living in corrosive melancholy, cruelty, violence and brutality? Are they familiar with the irrationalities and indignities that afflict the flesh and the spirit of man? Are they capable of sensing 'evanescence and brutality, vanity and rage, nothingness or hideous, useless hatred … cries suddenly stifled by silence, shadows engulfed forever in the night'? The crux of the issue is that by processing men through the Lasswellian models, we are leading humanity to tyranny of the worst kind. Who says that the Lasswellian models can help in understanding men, who are 'monkeys with the gift of speech', or 'bloody, ignorant apes', or a 'foul brood', whose 'life is just a mess, full of tall children grown stupider'. In fact, man is born into trouble, as the sparks fly upward, and 'it is a bad lookout for anyone in

Greek poetry when he is called a happy man'. The Lasswellian models fail to tame the demons of violence and coercion in human affairs. Their heady intoxication with research technologies has obscured the mission of political science. They have not only faltered in understanding human behaviour and political processes in the affluent countries of the West, but have proved equally meaningless in exposing the politics of closed societies, where the 'secret police hovers like guardian angels over men's spirits' and party bureaucracy extends its leviathan structure in all its harshness. They have also proved futile in examining the rise of the neo-despots and tin-pot dictators of the military regimes, where 'politics is an exercise of ventriloquism', that is, rulers speak on behalf of a populace, which is necessarily mute most of the time. As such, the whole of the Lasswellian edifice is built on false premises—it is aloof from the complexities of human nature and the realities of closed societies. One should, therefore, break the spell of Harold Lasswell, dismiss his phantom models and rewrite the script.

The Lasswellian models do not take root—they are not the heart and soul of human existence for they stand in the abyss of desolate alienation from the visions, prognostications and pledges of human delight. They are not only critical of philosophy, but equally ignorant of history, in the absence of which 'politics becomes a second-rate activity, neither an art nor a science, at once corrupting to the soul and fatiguing to the mind'. They lack the throb of life and are without faith, radiance or hope. They are incapable of guiding political theory across the boisterous seas of wars and violence, or the havens of truth and ahimsa, because in them there is neither destination nor attainment. These newfangled Lasswellian models of politics have led to reckless bandying of phrases torn out of their psychological context, which are incomprehensible to a political scientist because of their psycho-pathological connotations and to a psychologist because of a computerized transplanting into a singularly alien soil of politics. To be sure, there is a ring of stuffy pompousness and obscurity about Lasswellian phraseology. Imprisoned in the narrow cells of techniques, they have not been able to articulate a viable theory of human behaviour—its past, present and possible futures. Rooted in thought control systems and stereotyped motives, they will lead ultimately to stunted human faculties and diminished minds. Their retreat towards rigidity and the euphoria and desperate atmosphere created by them have dissolved ethical paradoxes, postulatory norms and critical judgement at a price some have not yet calculated. Submerged in an ocean of facts, they have created a dull, routine theory, which is increasingly sterile, formal and ceremonial, or 'a pretentious collection of trivialities'. Their 'theorizing activity' or computerized culture is unclear and ambiguous, enfeebled and superfluous, and so dwarfed by vacillation over the choice of ends and means that they are driving political science towards a shapeless monomania.

The Lasswellian models show poor understanding of the wretched of the earth and a mass of lumpen proletariat. As Robert A. Nisbet said: "If in renaissance thought, it was the myth of reasonable man which predominated; if in the eighteenth century, it was natural man; and in the nineteenth century, economic or political man, it is by no means unlikely that for our own age, it is alienated or maladjusted man who will appear to later historians as the key figure of twentieth century thought." This 'key figure' of Nisbet is vastly neglected in the Lasswellian models. They utterly fail to note the process of alienation and automatization in both capitalist and communist societies. It has been said: "In the nineteenth century, the problem was that God is dead; in the twentieth century, the problem is that man is dead. In the nineteenth century, inhumanity meant cruelty; in the twentieth century, it means schizoid self-alienation. The danger of the past was that men became slaves. The danger of the future is that men may become robots. True enough, robots do not rebel. But given man's nature, robots cannot live and remain sane—they become 'golems'; they will destroy their world and themselves because they cannot stand any longer the boredom of a meaningless life."[14] Thus, the Lasswellian models will lead ultimately to robotism, where man will be devoid of feeling and sensation. If man would choose the Lasswellian style, it would mean that he is opting for baleful and ruinous days, insanity and destruction—indeed history's most calamitous period. The mechanical models of Lasswell would inaugurate an era of spiritual poverty, dehumanization and eventual decay of culture. As such, they are likely to prove injurious and wasteful for the salubrious growth of political theory. One should not forget that man's faith in reason, goodwill and sanity require value premises. A small tribe was told thousands of years ago: "I put before you life and death, blessing and curse—and you choose any." They chose life, and the choice for us would be the same, but that spirit of life is handcuffed in the Lasswellian models. Let us not forget that 'the task of the generation now in rebellion is to reassert the authority of morality over technology'.[15] The Lasswellian shade is a veil of technology—it has not the slightest vision of morality. The wholesome and serene dimensions of political theory are so obscured and concealed under the medley mixture of technology that society is left without an organ of self-consciousness. As such, Lasswell may be the 'gadfly' of American behaviouralism, but he cannot claim to be a pioneer for humanity at large. His puerile models, uninteresting jargon and tedious vocabulary are too monotonous, bewildering and even peevish for a meaningful life. Teeming with techniques and overflowing with data laden slang, the Lasswellian models fail to promise an exciting journey or even a rewarding one. It is, therefore, time that we pack up the Lasswellian spectre and bid it farewell.

Lasswell has been unkind to political theory. He has enveloped political theory in technical gadgets and claws of data, so much so that its tender, gentle and humane chords have become sore. As such, the Lasswellian models hardly incite and instigate, or attract and allure, any sensible and purposeful oriented man. Let Lasswell remember that there is a difference between the light of a candle and that of a bright sun. Let him remember the old Russian fable that an eagle can sometimes fly lower than a chicken, but a chicken can never rise to the same heights as an eagle. His models, at their best, are no more than chicken models; they are by no stretch of the imagination eagle models. The light that they project, if any, is the light of a candle, through which the 'doyen' tries to dispel the darkness of caves. His models can't reshape life for they have never understood a thing about life—its breath, its palpitations and its throbs. His models look upon life as a lump of raw material which can be tested in a laboratory and processed by his touch. They imagine man as a cork floating on the ocean of society, but forget that he is a power for enriching and utilizing whatever the society might encompass. Let us remember that life is never a material, a substance to be moulded. If Lasswell wants to know, life is the principle of self-renewal, it is constantly renewing, changing and transfiguring itself; it is infinitely beyond his theories about it. As such, his models may be relevant for an artificial society, but certainly not for a free society, embedded in imaginative and adventurous programmes. His models even fail to restrain the 'idiot masses' and the 'crackpot realism' of the power elites, who have control over the final destiny of mankind. Neither do the Lasswellian models stimulate the growth of a 'sane society', nor do they promote the ideals of 'humanistic communitarianism', because they view man as a spiritual cripple. They see only the narrow limits of life, but fail to note that within its genial range, what rubies sparkle, what heavenly days befall, and what blessed moments supervene. Let Lasswell recollect what Henri Poincare once wrote: "Science is built with facts as a house is built with stones, but a collection of facts is no more science than a heap of stones is a house." Where facts are piled upon facts and hooked in a technical rigmarole, all sense of purpose is lost. A political theory shred of its humanizing compassion can hardly civilize and cultivate human beings; it would be mere submission to technology and, hence, brutalizing for mankind in the long run.

Thus, the whole argument is that cut off from values, morality and ethical premises, the behavioural ideology was moving on a forked support of value relativism. Its excessive attachment to methodology appeared crooked and wrinkled, its extreme orientation towards techniques began to dither and disintegrate, and its exponents soon found themselves stumbling with a crutch. Covered with crumbs of technical fantasy, its efforts to understand 'the observed and the observable' began to crumble into fragments. Staggering under the weight of its own techniques, its adherents were compelled to turn to new styles to understand human behaviour. Instead of according priority to techniques, they shouted the new slogan that 'substance must precede techniques'. Indeed, a noisy catchphrase or a new style to shield their deficiencies under the shelter of another movement, known as the post-behavioural revolution in political science.

Notes

1. Louis D. Hayes and Ronald D. Hedlund (eds). 1970. *The Conduct of Political Inquiry: Behavioural Political Analysis* (Englewood Cliffs, N.J., Prentice-Hall, Inc.) pp. 47–50.
2. Alfred De Grazia. 1962. *Political Behaviour Vol. I* (New York, The Free Press) p. 7.
3. Heinz Eulau. 1963. *The Behavioural Persuasion in Politics* (New York, Random House) p. 3, 140.
4. Mitchell and Mitchell. 1972. *Political Analysis and Public Policy: An Introduction to Political Science* (New Delhi, Thomson Press) p. vii.

5. W.H. Greenleaf. 1972. 'Theory and the Study of Politics', in *British Journal of Political Science*, Vol. 2, October, p. 469.
6 McCoy and Playford (eds). 1967. *Apolitical Politics* (New York, Thomas Y. Crowell) pp. 8–9.
7. Peter H. Odegard. 1969. *Political Power and Social Change* (Mumbai, Oxford and IBH Publishing House) p. 65.
8. Howard B. White. 1961. 'The Processed Voter and the New Political Science', in *Social Research,* Vol. 28, p. 127.
9. Martin Landau. 1972. *Political Theory and Political Science* (New York, The Macmillan Co.) p. 15.
10. H.R.G. Greaves. 1958. *The Foundations of Political Theory* (London, George Allen and Unwin), p. 7.
11. Michael Curtis (ed.). 1961. *The Great Political Theories Vol. 1* (New York, Avon Book Division) p. 21.
12. Hans J. Morgenthau. 1962. *The Decline of Democratic Politics* (Chicago, The University of Chicago Press) p. 31.
13. John W. Gardner. 1965. *Self-Renewal: The Individual and the Innovative Society* (New York, Harper Colophon Books) p. xiii.
14. Erich Fromm. 1959. *The Sane Society* (London, Routledge and Kegan Paul Ltd) p. 360.
15. Joan Robinson. 1970. *Freedom and Necessity: An Introduction to the Study of Society* (London, George Allen and Unwin Ltd.) p. 124.

4

The Credo of Relevance

The behavioural mode of political analysis resulted in formulating woolly, imprecise and bantam theories. It had 'too much precision misplaced on trivial matters, too little respect for crucial facts as against grand theories, too much respect for insights that are commonplace, too much indication and too little proof, too little genuine cumulation of generalizations, too little regard for the learning of the past, far too much jargon',[1] all of which have made researchers no more than mechanics tinkering with society. It is armed with a critical knowledge of neither history nor philosophy and, therefore, has not been able to explore the mysteries of political society. It confused history with a record of the past and likened it to the futile effort of transferring dead bones from one graveyard to another. It could not understand the wisdom of Will Durant's famous observation that 'the present is the past rolled up for action and the past is the present unrolled for understanding'. It could never realize that history is industry, history is art, and history is philosophy. It is industry in so far as it ferrets out facts; it is an art in so far as it reconstructs and interprets past events, ideas and institutions; it is philosophy in so far as it provides a perspective and enlightenment. The behavioural aloofness, even vehemence, against history led to the growth of unsatisfying general explanations and the piling up of a heap of 'bad theory' in politics. Its attempts to bid farewell to philosophy was a departing message to reason and humanism, by which it instilled the worst kind of 'occupational myopia' or 'empirical conservatism', in political theory. Its laissez-faire attitude toward political engagement and its 'abolition of man' allowed politics to degenerate into a kind of technology and drowned political theory in the gloom of value relativism. Its passionless mood and fondness for natural science paradigms, combined with its craze for ethical neutrality, led to increasing social and political crises. It faltered badly in providing a satisfactory answer to the malaise of our age. It hurriedly reached its dead end by the 1960s because of a number of blind and unquestioned ideological biases and its emphasis on rigour as paramount to relevance; its condition was like that of a sick and collapsing man, put in an oxygen chamber.

As such, its exponents, or 'the new American mandarins', were left with no alternative but to direct their energy and scholarship to face this new challenge and they 'reacted to the geometrically intensifying pragmatic problems of political existence'.[2] They quickly modified the tenets of behaviouralism so as to remove its symptoms of disease. This modified version led to the development of a new style in political theory in the form of post-behaviouralism, which is often referred to as a 'revolution'.

The post-behavioural revolution is styled as the 'new' and 'latest challenge'. Its battle cries are 'relevance' and 'action' and it appears to be 'a specific episode' in the history of political science. It unravels a deep dissatisfaction against the rigorously scientific methodology of the natural sciences. It appears to be just another reaction to 'behaviouralism', but with notable differences. It is considered to be 'future-oriented'. It does not try to conserve or even to destroy a particular methodological approach or to seek to return to some golden age of political research. It does not deny the possibility of discovering testable generalizations about human behaviour. It seeks to propel political science in new directions, by adopting a new technology. It prefers to add something to behaviouralism. It is neither a reaction, nor preservation, nor even a counter-reformation to behaviouralism. It is considered a genuine revolution or reform in political science. It is even styled as a movement and an intellectual tendency. As a movement, it includes in its fold different shades of exponents, ranging from conservatism to the active left. It is not a systematic movement, for it indicates 'diffuse, unstable and prickly qualities'. It is a broad, inchoate movement, without any particular methodological commitments. Its appeal is diversified, for it embraces rigorous scientists as well as dedicated classicists. Its adherents come from different age groups and from different styles of thought. "Its whole improbable diversity—political, methodological and generational—is bound together by one sentiment alone, a deep discontent with the direction of contemporary political research."

Post-behaviouralism is equally an intellectual tendency or style. Its intellectual components form the tenets of its faith and are often called 'a credo of relevance'. David Easton has enumerated the basic characteristics of post-behaviouralism in his presidential address at the 65th meeting of the American Political Science Association in September 1965. Its first tenet is that 'substance must precede technique'. It is more significant to be relevant and meaningful for contemporary social problems than to be sophisticated in the tools of investigation. Mere sophistication of techniques will not do; substance is equally and, often, even more relevant for the study of problems and issues. It prefers to say that 'it is better to be vague than non-relevantly precise'—a dictum that has uprooted the behavioural aphorism of science, which states that 'it is better to be wrong than vague'. Its second article of faith is that 'behavioural science conceals an ideology of empirical conservatism' and it would be wrong to confine oneself exclusively to the description and analysis of facts, as that could hamper the understanding of the same facts in their broadest context. It advocates that empirical political science must lend its support to the maintenance of the very factual conditions it explores. It unwittingly purveys an ideology of social conservatism tempered by modest incremental change. Its third feature is a devastating blow to behaviouralism. It upholds that behaviouralism has lost touch with reality, for the essence of its inquiry is 'abstraction and analysis' and this serves to conceal the brute realities of politics. Its task, therefore, is 'to break the barriers of silence that behavioural language has necessarily created and to help political science reach out to the real needs of mankind in a time of crisis'. Its fourth characteristic is that constructive development of values is an inextinguishable part of the study of politics. It is difficult for science to be evaluatively neutral and, hence, awareness of the value premises is necessary to understand the limits of our knowledge and the alternatives for which this knowledge could be used. Its fifth attribute is a reminder to the intellectuals of their unique task, obligation and historical role. It says that intellectuals ought to protect the humane values of civilization, otherwise they will be reduced to mere technicians or mechanics tinkering with society. Its sixth feature is styled as 'action science', the purpose of which is to reflect the contemporary conflict in society over ideals and this must permeate and colour the whole research enterprise itself. Lastly, intellectuals have the obligation to implement their knowledge—they cannot stand apart from the struggles of the day. As such, politicization of professions is both inescapable and desirable. These, then, are the broad features of the credo of relevance, or post-behaviouralism, though its exponents differ on some of these views.[3]

As already indicated, there were several factors for the rise of post-behaviouralism. The behavioural movement had shown its weaknesses in understanding the agony of the present social crisis. Its 'acknowledged glacial pace and apparent remoteness' could not meet the demands that arose in the contexts of social and economic crises. It failed to touch the fear of the nuclear bomb, mounting internal cleavages in the US, the war in Vietnam that violated the 'moral conscience' of the world, the devastating population explosion, dangerous pollution of the environment, racial and economic dissent, increasing social conflict and deepening fears and anxieties about the future. In the face of a human situation such as this, the post-behavioural movement has tried to present a new image and the obligations of political theory. It need not be considered 'a threat to behavioural research, but only an extension of it necessary for coping with the unusual problems of the present epoch'. It pleads for more relevant research to prescribe and to act so as to improve political life according to human criteria. It deplores what it views as technical excesses in research, yet it adheres to the view that technical adequacy is vital. It makes some objections to scientific abstractness and remoteness from the world of commonsense, yet at the same time insists that science by its very nature must deal with abstractions. It asserts: "No science could by itself cope with the whole reality as it is interpreted by the politician." Only by analysis, by chopping the world up into manageable units of inquiry, by precision achieved through measurement wherever possible, can political science meet the continuing needs of a complex, post-industrial society for more reliable knowledge. As such, its exponents say: "Today, we need to temper our behavioural image of the discipline so that in these critical times, we no longer see it as commanding us to devote most of our efforts to the discovery of demonstrable basic truths about politics. We will need to obtain more of our satisfactions from seeking immediate answers to immediate problems." The nature of post-behaviouralism as such, lies not in the rejection of the scientific method per se, but in the recognition of its limits. It continues to value precision and verifiability as scholarly traits, but they have been wedded to a spirit of critical method. "If the pre-behavioural era was characterized by critical independence without precision, and the behavioural era by precision without criticism, the 'cunning of reason' has seen fit to affect an *Aufhebung* of these approaches in the post-behavioural era: that is, precision with criticism."

The post-behaviouralists are equally divided about the contents of this movement. One school prefers the abandonment of science altogether because of the present fear of physical and political self-destruction. Its adherents say that science is simply incapable of measuring up to contemporary needs. To them, science is defective and convictions are more important. The second school continues to place its hopes in modern behavioural science and concludes that they have no alternative but to make their research more relevant. They can do this by devoting all their professional energies to research, prescription and action with regard to the immediate issues of the day.

But there is a common message underlying the constant post-behavioural complaint against behaviouralism. It is argued that behaviouralist research is not relevant, that excessive preoccupation with techniques and factual description has distracted behaviouralists from significant questions about the operation of the American democratic system in particular. Its research myopia has discouraged us from posing the right questions for discovering the basic forces that shape the making and execution of authoritative decisions. This is an indirect warning to behaviouralists that all research, whether pure or applied, of necessity rests on certain value assumptions. It is a myth that research can be value free or neutral. As such, post-behaviouralism upholds that our operating values be brought forward for self-conscious examination and that their impact on research be assessed. It recognizes the hazards of neglecting normative presuppositions. It is a plea to broaden the vision of our basic research and to end our hesitation towards normative premises. It discards the narrow vision of ethical neutrality and promises to examine the extent to which values determine the selection of problems and their ultimate interpretations.

Post-behaviouralism has led to the growth of a reconciliation approach in political theory. This is visible in the writings of a number of contemporary political thinkers. It would perhape be desirable to give a passing reference to the ideas of reconciliation as formulated by William T. Bluhm, Eugene J. Meehan, Andrew Hacker, George Catlin, Thomas A. Spragens, Jr, Fred M. Frohock and Bernard Crick.

William T. Bluhm,[4] in his book, *Theories of the Political System*, takes this form of presentation: comparisons of new and old—of modern students of politics with classical writers. His argument proceeds from the premise that modern political studies are already informed and made sophisticated by the classics. Classical theories furnish the foundations of nearly all the work that is being done today in the field of politics. What he describes is not a return to the classical truth and to tradition, but a moving forward from what is true in the classics and usable in tradition. Each persuasion claims to be the sole orthodoxy, yet each gives us insights into only some aspects of politics and neglects the whole. What is required is synthesis, the building of bridges from theory to theory. He hopes that a comparative review of the classical theories in the context of this problem, and of the modern studies which build on them, may bring us some way on the road to such a goal. He pleads that pure scientific description in the case of man and society is not possible at any very general level and that science must involve ethics, if it is not to become description masquerading as ideology. In alliance with students of values, however, as helpmates in the quest for human nature and the prediction of its consequences (its fulfilment), the building of scientific models and their application to empirical situations can be of deep significance for human enterprise. Instead of ideology, this science becomes, in the broadest and best sense, philosophy. There is, thus, Bluhm says, a need for philosophical science (science to involve ethics) and scientific philosophy (theory getting help from scientific methods) for understanding human nature and for the building of bridges from theory to theory.

Similarly, Eugene J. Meehan[5] starts with the idea of systematic inquiry as an operation that requires the use of various tools or instruments. These tools can be tested only in use. Explanations are such tools and they provide people with the means of control over their environment. Value judgements are also tools—they provide people with the means of choosing between alternative courses of action. In using explanations, people engage in empirical inquiry. Neither of these forms of inquiry can be separated from the other. In both of them, the instruments—the explanations and value judgements—are created by men to fulfil their purposes and, in both of them, the test of adequacy of the instruments lies in practice. As such, Meehan pleads for a political theory that could provide an effective way for circumventing the gap between fact and value in social sciences.

Another distinguished authority, Andrew Hacker[6], pleads for close cooperation between the normative and empirical political theories. He enumerates the utility of both the traditional and contemporary concepts of political theory and says that there are few bridges between them. The reasons, he writes, are not hard to find. Research in the two fields is generally conducted by scholars of different temperaments and interests. One group is concerned with the development of ideas over an extended period of time, the other is intent on discovering and ordering the facts of contemporary political life. One group defines scholarship as a detailed understanding of the greater and lesser texts of an intellectual tradition, the other sees research in terms of first-hand investigation of the real world and conceptual rigour in the handling of the facts. Hacker says that the differences and tensions between these two approaches to theory, in a very large measure, are based on the ignorance of what the other is trying to do. He, therefore, pleads for closer collaboration and communication between the value-laden and empirical conceptions of political theory.

Another equally conspicuous theorist, George Catlin[7], although he had 'personally been more concerned with political and ethical philosophy than with political science', nevertheless quoted too much in almost scholastic style in his renowned study, *Systematic Politics*: He restates the position that in building a scientific theory, what matters is not the claim or dispute about originality, but to build up the structure, brick by brick, on well-laid foundations. He takes 'political science seriously' and stresses upon the separation in political theory between political science and political philosophy. To build a coherent and systematic political theory, he pleads for a far more fundamental structural analysis of political science, but at the same time puts forward 'the valuational issues of the day'. The general impression that one gathers after reading *Systematic Politics* is that although Catlin's emphasis is on systematic political theory, he has not totally ignored the valuational issues either.

Another contemporary theorist, Thomas A. Spragens, Jr.[8], highlights the fact that the bifurcation of political theory into separate normative and empirical halves has created significant anomalies in the conceptual structure of political science. Maintaining that this separation must be overcome, Spragens explores the basic assumptions behind compartmentalization and outlines a paradigm for the reintegration of political theory in the post-behavioural science of politics. The conceptual structure of contemporary political theory and the fundamental concepts that order our thought and research are unsatisfactory. At the worst, he characterizes the situation as a 'crisis'. The principal manifestation of this intellectual difficulty at the level of the practising political scientist is the barrenness of theorizing that relentlessly and rigidly tries to maintain the alleged hiatus between empirical and normative theory. Already the most penetrating minds of the discipline are beginning to suggest that the divorce was too hasty and that some sort of reconciliation is possible. Spragens shares the feeling that if the empirical and normative theories have nothing to say to each other, ultimately, they will have nothing to say. As such, he pleads for the reconciliation and reintegration of the two. This 'reintegration of the theoretical enterprise in political science is a necessity because politics is the intersection of order and power. The latter cannot be wholly abstracted from the former, however diligent the effort, and the former cannot be described apart from patterns and standards, which are perceptual, interpretative norms'. He, therefore, draws our attention to this dilemma in contemporary political theory and resurrects the relevance and meaningful quality of values in political life.

The views of Fred M. Frohock are of great concern. In his earlier book, *The Nature of Political Inquiry*,[9] Frohock discloses the tacit dimensions of political theory and weighs the stakes involved in choosing between the positivist and metaphysical epistemologies. He rejects the claims of methodological superiority of both extreme positivism and pure metaphysics. He asserts that the application of scientific methods to limited areas of political inquiry may be worthwhile, yet in risking the loss of 'the distinctiveness of social phenomena', we pay a high price for its adoption. Frohock thus accepts a version of the positivist view that meaningful analytical distinctions can be made between facts and values and opts for a modified emptive theory of value. He adjudicates the fact–value question, permits political scientists a fair measure of short-run value neutrality, determines the status of ethical statements, and defends an emotivist theory of values. He concludes with a definition of politics and exhorts political scientists to undertake empirical studies of socialization and to develop an empirical theory of value. The reader is left with the impression of a tidy, straightforward, perhaps somewhat sombre, summary of current 'middle of the road' epistemological preoccupations in contemporary political science. In his later book, *Normative Political Theory*,[10] Frohock comes out more openly in defence of normative theory and states that 'philosophy, while not guaranteed to settle anything, will at least clarify the criteria by which claims can be settled'. The contemporary issues of academic freedom, research objectivity, participation in politics and the research for relevance, Frohock argues, have 'philosophical roots which must be unearthed if the issues are to be discussed sensibly'. He arrives at the conclusion that 'normative inquiry is not paralysed by the positivist thesis on values once the deficiencies of this thesis are revealed, and normative inquiry is as amenable to systematic or rigorous exploration as any of the empirical modes of political inquiry', and that 'normative political theory is neither dead nor dying, but rather alive and rich with possibilities'. Frohock has thus not only criticized positivism, but also vindicated the 'normative concerns' of traditional political philosophy.

A similar defence has been taken by Bernard Crick[11] in *Political Theory and Practice*. Crick's provocative insights are philosophical and traditional. He emphasizes the proper role of political theory in the service of politics—in normative choice, action and, indeed, political existence. He defines politics as 'the art of the possible'—with 'possible' meaning 'the interplay between a tradition of behaviour and theories and doctrines'—of separating and reintegrating theory and doctrine—'with fact–value linked to recognition of problematic selection among alternative possibilities'.

All these political thinkers are more impressive because they see, or choose to see, that the task of reintegration, or the creation of a new political synthesis, is the main riddle confronting political theory today. They call attention to the basic proposition that 'if a man fails to consider moral and political questions seriously, he may reduce himself and his progeny to an ugly and distasteful, if not brutal, animality'[12] and, as such, 'in politics, empirical inquiry without a philosophic framework must needs be blind, as political philosophy, without empirical verification, must needs be wholly speculative'. Unsupported by empirical theory, traditional theory would be inarticulate and fragmentary, and cut off from a philosophical base, empirical theory would be feckless and ready to dodder and evanesce. What is needed is a new creative political theory based on 'precision with criticism', which means flourishing within the genial range of normative and empirical fields, discarding 'is-ought' disjunctions and evaluating the results in the light of ideals, and ideals in the light of results. Then alone would political theory be able 'to explain and predict—to establish relationships between thought and action, means and ends, cause and effect, conditions and consequences',[13] or, in Hobbes' words, be able to gain and impart 'knowledge of consequences and dependence of one fact upon another'. Then alone could a political theory 'sensitively respond' to the urgent problems of society and to the emerging social needs and be able to articulate a sophisticated system of values and 'provide once again a bridge between the needs of society and the knowledge of social sciences'.

It seems that post-behaviouralism, which is directed against a developing behavioural orthodoxy and whose battle cries are 'relevance and action', is a raving, rambling structure without any ultimate destiny. It is a phrase trotted out to indicate that the behavioural movement has reached a dead end and that, while a serious effort is being made to synthesize the traditional, behaviouralism is the proverbial red herring in its way. In its attempts to embrace rigorous scientists as well as dedicated classicists, it falters badly. Its efforts to make political theory future oriented have many diffuse, unstable and even prickly qualities. Its 'credo of relevance' is merely a catchphrase that raises a number of difficult questions regarding professional ethics and values, the relationship between science and society, freedom of inquiry, and the relationship between government and the scholarly community. It has not helped political science to have to face mounting internal cleavages and stark inequalities, violent protests and secret movements, fear of the nuclear bomb and the devastating population explosion, excessive political repression and abuse of power, racial hatred and untouchability, eclipse of social justice and the curtailment of individual freedom, and related issues. Its central tenets that 'substance must precede technique' and that 'it is better to be vague than non-relevantly precise', its emphasis on the intellectuals' historical role in protecting the human values of civilization, its awareness of value premises and bold speculative theorizing, and its prescription to improve political life according to human criteria and its highlighting of the significance of knowledge are all nothing but caricatured classical political theory. Its attempts to purport 'modest incremental change' in the behavioural ideology of 'social conservatism' and thereafter to mingle the whole carcass of rigorous techniques with values, seems to be drivel. It is an inchoate movement full of oddities for it neither seeks to return to the so-called 'golden age' of political research nor to conserve or even destroy a particular methodological approach. Neither does it have committed theorists or groups in its fold, nor has it any particular methodological commitments. With its heterogeneous adherents, ranging widely from conservatism to the active left, it has driven political theory towards a new crisis. Its exponents are only bound together by one sentiment—a deep discontent with the direction of contemporary political research. It is at its best a negative unity, a passing phenomenon, a kind of accident of history that will somehow fade away soon.

Both behaviouralism and post-behaviouralism have not been successful in establishing explanatory laws, as compared to the older and better known generalizations arrived at in traditional political theory. One example is Karl Marx's theory that a change from one form of society to another is always the result of class struggle, which, in turn, is ultimately due to changes in the 'forces of production', that is, in the materials or tools or types of labour used to produce goods. Marxism is a social philosophy that explains in the most scientific fashion the laws of social change and the direction such changes will inevitably take in the future. It presents a classic machinery for thinking about man, society and history. It describes a total social structure and that too in historical motion. What is central in Marxism is the capacity and willingness to look beyond immediately observable facts and see the tree of the future in the tiny, barely perceptible shoots of the present. It is the combination of historical vision and the courage to be utopian—with the vision sternly disciplined by an analysis of tendencies discernible at the present time and with the utopia rendered concrete by the identification of the social forces that may be expected to further its realization. Whatever be its limitations, Marxism is a powerful magnifying glass under which the irrationality of the capitalist system protrudes in all of its monstrous forms. The Marxist approach may not be an infallible method of studying politics, but it would surely be a great improvement upon the existing scientific theories if conjoined with a systematic study of history and philosophy. The most remarkable thing about Marxism is that despite being scientific, it is suffused with humanism—it is the social womb of the 'new man'. Behaviouralism and post-behaviouralism have never sought such answers and, therefore, have none to offer.

Post-behaviouralism, with all its emphasis that substance must precede technique, that behavioural research must not lose touch with reality and that knowledge must be implemented, has not been able to produce enduring basic changes in political science's intellectual and methodological underpinnings. In its attempts to support behavioural methods and techniques and to make their substantive implications more cogent, it has been swinging up and down, tossing to and fro, sometimes going backward into the past, and sometimes projecting into the future. Its lack of finality over intellectual issues, reliance on conceptual schemes from such disciplines as economics, sociology and psychology, and gazing at the political cleavages of the late 1960s and the 1970s have all left scars on the character and status of political theory. It has attempted to derive its food for thought from a number of contemporary definitions of political theory, which often overlap and are bewildering. For example, one writer in the beginning of the 20th century said that political science was the study of the State and the 'realization of the State will' and he viewed political theory as a special discipline concerned with the authorities that express that will and with ideas in and about politics. Another writer distinguished three related elements of political theory—historical, analytical and applied. A third stuck to the belief that the basic aim in political theory was not pure science, but the 'cross-fertilization of politics with science' and the goal of political science was to 'interpret and explain and measurably control the forces of human nature'. A fourth maintained that 'the greatest need of the hour is the development of a scientific technique and methodology for political science'. A fifth suggested that political theory consisted of three logically distinct kinds of propositions—factual, causal and valuational. A sixth claimed that political scientists should 'leave ethics to the philosophers and concern themselves primarily with the description and analysis of political behaviour'. A seventh noticed an emerging sense of a deep cleavage in terms of philosophical reflection as opposed to logical analysis, the theological approach versus the empirical, and the conflict between the philosophy of history and an emphasis on the ends–means relationship. An eighth said that the basic purpose of political theory was 'to decrease the indeterminancy of important political judgements' and enhance the changes for a rational democratic society. A ninth said that theory had entered upon a time of trouble because some saw it as a 'historical, reflective and literary discipline more akin to moral philosophy', while others viewed it as a set of systematic generalizations for dealing with empirical data. A tenth said that 'political theory is dead because in communist countries, it is imprisoned; elsewhere it is moribund'. An eleventh pondered over the causes of decline as part of the syndrome of post-enlightenment thought. A twelfth boldly spoke of the 'revival' of political theory and emphasized that it would not wholly perish from the earth. And, a thirteenth sounded a new theory chorus based on a recommitment to the goals of science, or a coherent image of the political system, or the idea of political science as a policy science. It is against this background that post-behaviouralism attempts to build the possibility of 'political engineering in American culture'. It represents an ideological critique of the field as it was in the late 1960s and a philosophical critique of the behavioural image of science. It is more a condition or a name for less than coherent congeries of interests than an intelligible intellectual movement or even mood. It is a concept that means many things and one hardly knows its exact meaning, except its emphasis on policy science. In its attempts to gather together the dispersed threads of political theory, it has become a mongrel creed and does not tell us where we are. One post-behavioural writer would announce an end to the conflict between 'humanists' and the 'science establishment' and herald a 'paradigm synthesis'. A second believes that there is not only a need for more 'organizational boundary crossing' between political science and political philosophy, but 'a need to improve the quantity and quality of discussion across the different schools that have gradually established enclaves in political theory'. A third equates post-behaviouralism with post-positivism and asks whether there is life for scientific theory beyond positivism. A fourth suggests that 'we are coming to the end of an era in political science, a slow, whimpering end', which indicates that 'the hoped for cumulation of knowledge into a coherent body of theory has not occurred'. A fifth has noted that post-behaviouralism lacks a provocative vision and such a vision has never been indigenous to American political science. As such, it could be said that American post-behaviouralism has not been able to cultivate novel ideas. It has only been a 'domesticator' and, as such, the direction of political theory has not been altered fundamentally. Neither has it been able to understand the relationship between political science and politics, nor has it been able to establish a liaison between the political scientists and the policy elites, nor to state exactly the form of interaction between public and academic discourse and the vehicle of that interaction. It has not successfully brought 'political science into a new age of intellectual ferment and maturity as a discipline, nor evolved it into a conceptually coherent scholarly enterprise'. It does not demonstrate any great ability to transcend American political culture, or any other culture, and it is highly unlikely that a unifying vision of political theory can emerge from this material. Though it has been able to establish a very few 'partial equilibria' and theories of 'heresthetics', its methodology has failed so far to make serious theoretical progress on any of the major issues facing political science. It has done nothing remotely comparable to the psychologists who invented factor analysis and scaling methods to cope with mental tests; or the economists who created structural equation estimation to deal with their models, especially the economy-wide macroeconomic theories; or even the sociologists who have contributed latent class analysis to the corpus of social scientific methodology. It has merely tried to transplant these models in political science, which is why it has not been able to establish hegemony and become the 'predominant paradigm'. It has become increasingly clear that its search for a single paradigm is futile because it has been missing the real core of human life. It has hardly paid any attention to the saying of Charles Darwin, when he writes: "But for many years I cannot endure to read a line of poetry. My mind seems to have become a kind of machine for grinding laws out of a large collection of facts, but why this should have caused the atrophy of that part of the brain on which tastes depend, I cannot conceive. The loss of these tastes is a loss of happiness, and may possibly be injurious to the intellect, and more probably to the moral character, by enfeebling the emotional part of our nature." As such, because of its similarity to behavioural methodology, post-behaviouralism has left unresolved the intellectual issues and finer tastes of human life.

The post-behavioural efforts to reintegrate science and philosophy may look glamorous on paper, but have proved unrealizable in practice. Post-behaviouralism has not been able to take upon, to use Bentham's phrase, the task of the 'expositor and that of the censor', or to reintegrate the political scientist and the political philosopher, or the realms of science (relevance) and those of morals and values. It has not succeeded in breaking sharply the behavioural professional paradigm about the moral relationship between research and action. Its boundaries between pure research and service continue to be blurred and knowledge often seems divorced from action. It has neither returned to the humanistic conception of political science, nor abandoned the empirical tone of behaviouralism. It has put the talents of political scientists largely in the service of the elites in society and neglected the huge mass of mankind, resulting in the growth of an imbalance in political studies. It has extended behavioural methods and techniques.

Post-behaviouralists ought to remember that it is well nigh impossible to develop a well-integrated field in political theory. They should realize that 'there can be no conclusion to a book on political theory'. All that is possible is 'to clear up one or two loose ends'. Let them recollect the wisdom of what Oakeshott once said: "In political activity, then, men sail a boundless and bottomless sea; there is neither harbour for shelter nor floor for anchorage, neither starting place nor appointed destination."[14] As such, nothing is evaluated in post-behaviouralism, nothing is explained, for it falters on Goethe's criterion: "Theory is grey, while the tree of life is evergreen."

Notes

1. Berelson and Steiner. 1964. *Human Behaviour: An Inventory of Scientific Findings* (New York, Harcourt Brace World) p. 12.
2. David Easton. 1969. 'The New Revolution in Political Science', in *American Political Science Review,* 63, pp. 1051–61.
3. David Easton. 1970 'The New Revolution in Political Science', in *Approaches to the Study of Political Science,* (eds) Michael Hass and Henry S. Kariel (Scranton, Chandlar Publishing Co.) pp. 511–29
4. William T. Bluhm. 1971. *Theories of the Political System* (Englewood Cliffs, N.J., Prentice Hall, Inc.).
5. Eugene J. Meehan. 1971. *The Foundations of Political Analysis: Empirical and Normative* (Homewood, Ill., The Dorsey Press).
6. Andrew Hacker. 1968. *Political Theory: Philosophy, Ideology, Science* (New York, The Macmillan Co.).
7. George E. Catlin. 1962. *Systematic Politics* (London, George Allen and Unwin Ltd).
8. Thomas A. Spragens, Jr. 1973. *The Dilemma of Contemporary Political Theory: Toward a Post-behavioural Science of Politics* (New York, Dunellen).
9. Fred M. Frohock. 1967. *The Nature of Political Inquiry* (Homewood, Ill., The Dorsey Press).
10. Fred M. Frohock. 1974. *Normative Political Theory* (Englewood Cliffs, N.J., Prentice-Hall, Inc.).
11. Bernard Crick. 1974. *Political Theory and Practice* (New York, Basic Books).

12. Morton A. Kaplan. 1970. *Dissent and the State in Peace and War* (New York, The Dunellen Co., Inc.) p. xiv.
13. Vernon Van Dyke. 1962. *Political Science: A Philosophical Analysis* (Stanford, Stanford University Press) p. 4.
14. Douglas V. Verney. 1965. *The Analysis of Political Systems* (London, Routledge and Kegan Paul Ltd) p. 200.

5

The Central Style in Political Theory

Political theory is littered with endless controversies, illusions and paradoxes. Its riddles are perplexing and indeed lie in a tangled state. The reverberations of the new science of politics, or the behavioural persuasions in politics, have been felt inevitably in political studies. It has transformed the texture of political theory and raised several controversies and challenges. The keynote of the behavioural movement is reflected in the writings of Heinz Eulau, who says: "What the behavioural persuasion challenges in the traditional study of politics, if it challenges anything, is the comfortable assumption that the theory is the same thing as knowledge. But theory is only a tool. Like all tools, it tends periodically to wear out and need replacement."[1] Elsewhere, Eulau writes, "Political science has studied political ideas, values, customs, symbols, institutions, processes and policies without reference to their creators for a long time, but the cost has been high."[2] Equating theory with a 'tool' and the saying that till the contemporary period, political science had been studied 'without reference to their creators'—both these assertions are faulty and fragile. The behavioural approach in politics is directed to the growth of the neutral, objective science of politics and the erosion of values. The value-laden political theory has been the first casualty in the behavioural onslaught. The rise of scientific–empirical inquiry and the subsequent deluge of the behavioural and Lasswellian models in the contemporary period have put a pallid covering over the grand traditions of philosophy, humanism and values. A denser mist of fact loaded language and a larger heap of data is rolling over the domain of political theory. The pedantic, grammatical rules of methodology and its panoply of facts, terminology, symbols and semantics have been mercilessly injected into political theory. The exponents of the rigorous science of politics have plundered and robbed systematically the majestic course of values. The dogged persistence of the behaviouralists and their organized pogrom have led astray the creativity and richness of the canonical writings of the past, or the philosophical analysis of the political phenomenon. Through a maze of perplexing data and a plethora of facts, it seems that the first rate intelligence and enormous moral self-confidence of the value-laden theory is in peril. Their ferocious passion for factual knowledge and false concern for relevance have led behaviouralists to construct spineless paradigms, concepts and generalizations in political theory. The behavioural professionalism in political theory has generated specialized, often trivial, research projects as well as the esoteric idiom of people who chatter mainly among themselves. And, the public stage is now occupied by the practitioners of a pseudo-scientific psephology, who impart their vacuous punditry to a largely indifferent audience. The whole predicament revolves around the issue that what was once at the centre (values) of political theory has now been pushed to the periphery, and what was in the periphery (facts) has been thrust in its place. This re-shifting of positions has created the worst type of tension in political theory. Value-laden political theory is, therefore, in urgent need of a rescue mission.

A study of this centre–periphery controversy in political theory is of utmost importance. It is by attending carefully to the value-laden theory that one can establish the historical identity of ideas and political wisdom and thereby enliven theory itself. Political theory today must question the fit between modern institutions and the conceptions of the good life that govern the age; it must confront the orientations of self, truth, rationality, compassion, the common good, politics and authority that define contemporary discourse. These issues must be explored with the support of value-laden premises. Only a 'noble science of politics' rooted in values and ethical considerations will ensure the buoyancy of history and lead to a 'society of gentlemen'. It is, therefore, the purpose of this essay to restate that values ought to be at the centre of political inquiry, instead of being pushed to the periphery.

The Segmental Classification of Political Theory

Political theory can be classified into two broad segments. Often, those who use the term, 'political theory', do not themselves seem to know what meaning they intend to convey and, quite commonly, those who do make their meaning clear disagree with each other. In fact, the interests and commitments of those engaged in political theorizing are varied and diffused. Broadly speaking, political theory can be segmented into two halves—value-laden and factual theory. This controversy is referred to as the value-fact dichotomy or ethical neutrality. The first segmentation of political theory, used in a traditional sense, relates to political thought, political speculation, political ideas or 'philosophizing about government'. It is a synonym for thoughts, conjectures and the grand philosophical tradition, extending from Plato to Marx, or even Laski. The traditional greats in political theory were interested in politics as part of a comprehensive form of inquiry and always described and discussed it in a rather elaborate context. They had a deep interest in matters of ethical and normative judgement. This included 'concepts of politics almost totally oriented to the political community as an abstraction, towards legal authority and the institutions exercising it, and towards the proper relationship between the political order and the good life'.[3] It was dominated by values and philosophy and the philosophers were concerned with 'ideal models', rather than 'process models'. It dealt more elaborately with the questions of 'prescription and evaluation' and focused attention on the problem of 'what ought to be', rather than 'what actually happened'. It revolved around the themes of potentiality and completion, the individual and his social fulfilment. It did not interest itself in causal theory and adhered to the 'analysis of the moral, rather than of the strictly empirical world'. Values had stood at the peak of normative theory's hierarchy of priorities. In fact, values had been the central concern of political inquiry.

The second segmentation of political theory is more closely associated with the term, 'scientific-empirical political theory'. Empirical theory is primarily interested in developing terms that 'have a firm empirical basis and are ideally measurable and operational'.[4] It is an explanatory theory, struggling to develop major tools of scientific explanation, laws and theories. It is a causal theory, or a body of laws and generalizations, concerning political activity, established by scientific technique and with scientific rigour. It is an explanatory tool for a political phenomenon, 'a summary statement of what we think we know about the explanation of a phenomenon'.[5] It challenges the comfortable assumption that theory is the same thing as knowledge. It says that theory is only a tool and its focus of attention is the 'observed and observable' behaviour of man. It tries to develop rigorous research designs and to apply precise methods of analysis to political behaviour problems. It is an attempt to construct systematic theory and is in search of reliable knowledge about empirical political phenomena. Its major import has been the self-conscious acceptance and application of models, both analytically in constructing theory and empirically in guiding research. It is confronted with the need to recognize that scientific understanding of political life is ultimately possible only by classifying the broad theoretical premises of research. It has come to focus on research on actualities, that is, on the disclosure of facts and of their interrelations, basing its findings of pains-taking observation and measurement, especially on a rapidly growing stock of pertinent statistics. It is a flight away from dogma—it is a quest for reality. Its quest for more scientific politics could easily be described as the paramount development in contemporary political theory. Today, the empirical trend is visible in the writings of leading political scientists. Several leading political science journals now carry mostly empirically inspired articles. Most of the elected officialdom of the American Political Science Association has increasingly tended to be composed of persons prominent in empirical writings, as, for example, Harold Lasswell, V.O. Key, Charles S. Hyneman, David Truman, Gabriel Almond, Robert Dahl, David Easton, Karl Deutsch, and one can often hear technical jargon concerning the improvement of research tools The dramatic changes in the vocabulary of contemporary political theory, an increased attention to analytic theory and quantitative techniques, and the concern for micro level studies and for interaction and system level problems, are all the result of behaviouralism. The empirical creed has left its mark on almost every specialization within contemporary political theory.

For more than a generation, the exponents of empirical political theory have been engaged in the study of politics, political systems, political culture, political institutions and political behaviour with impressive rapidity. Under its impact, the field of research strategies and techniques has proliferated remarkably. Universities and institutions are training researchers of political inquiry in the most effective techniques of data collection, processing and interpretation. The courses in research methods and quasi-experimental and experimental designs are multiplying throughout the discipline of political science, like monkeys in a rainforest. It is this rise and growth of empirical political theory that has put the 'value theory' in shambles. Its categorization of the value theory as a 'bottomless morass' has practically evaporated the 'conscience' out of political studies. When the adherents of causal theory use words such as 'decline', 'demise' and 'putrefaction' to denote the state of affairs, it is a clear indication that value theory has been pushed to the periphery. One authority speaks of value theory as one of the 'most neglected branches of philosophy'. Another delivers it a premature funeral oration, by saying: "In the English speaking world, where so many of the interesting political problems have been solved (at least superficially), political theory (normative) is dead. In the Communist countries, it is imprisoned. Elsewhere, it is moribund." A third states bluntly, "Justified or not, it is certainly a current view that there have recently been no significant contributions to political theory (political philosophy) either in England or America." A fourth dismisses it 'as peripheral to the study of the real political world'. A fifth styles it 'as immense piles of philosophic rubbish, accumulated from over two millennia of speculation', and hence its study is neither relevant to contemporary scholarship nor to contemporary politics. The real tragedy in political theory is that values have been pushed towards the circumference. Here then is the dilemma: The value theory is no longer at the centre of the discipline of political science—it has been hurled towards the surface.

And what was in the periphery (facts) has come to occupy the central position in political studies. This shifting of positions has created a crisis of a huge magnitude.

Politics, Human Nature and Political Betterment

The centre–periphery controversy in political theory is closely related to the meaning of politics, its purpose and human nature. Contemporary writers have interpreted 'politics 'in a rather different way. The contemporary definitions of 'politics' have their utility, but a big drawback is their clinical approach towards the study of political phenomena. One authority says, "Politics is the authoritative allocation of values in a community."[6] Another writes, "Politics is the struggle for power."[7] A third says, "Politics is a systematic effort to move other men in the pursuit of other designs."[8] A fourth explains, "Politics is who gets what, when, how."[9] These definitions of politics are not self-contained. They have severe limitations, if we dare to explore human nature and the complex activities of politics.

First, the above definitions do not undertake a comprehensive view of human nature. It is extremely difficult to derive uniform regularities and generalizations about human beings and their nature. Human beings, as we know them, are often selfish, but sometimes unselfish; their judgement is fallible, but sometimes in the course of an argument, different people come to hold the same view, which is, as far as we can see, reasonable and right; they are infinite in their complexity and aspirations, but finite in their capacities and achievements; they have values that are neither necessarily the same for all, nor actually different for each; they can help one another, and need to, but can hurt one another, and often do.[10] Each man, if he is to be a man, and conscious of himself as an agent and not merely a puppet, must have some angle in life that is peculiarly his, some realm of choices that is under his own control and, therefore, likely to be different from those that others might have chosen.[11] The great philosopher, Kant, thinks that it is the duty of the philosopher to believe and argue that men will improve in the end. Man has risen from 'the uttermost barbarian to the highest degree of skill'. It seems that 'nature has worked more with a view to man's rational self-esteem than to his mere well-being'. Kant writes that 'men are unsociable sociable beings' and are in search of a civil society, 'which can administer justice universally'.[12] Men are continually in search of free thought. Free thought has no beginning and no end. Or, rather, its beginning is lost in the thickets of prehistory and only the extinction of higher forms of life will see its end.[13] Throughout history, men have guided the general political movements and transformations by a type of political thought known as 'political idealism' and a counter type of thought and political action called 'political realism'.[14] A writer is of the view that "Like the forms of the physical world, the dreams of men spread and colonize their inner world, clash, excite, modify and destroy each other or preserve their stability by making strange accommodations with their rivals." Viewing the bewildering variety and changeability of the interests and standards which govern human behaviour, it seems that the efforts made by the exponents of 'scientific politics' to simplify them into mechanical uniformities, is most futile and hazardous. The definitions of 'politics', as given by David Easton, Max Weber, Bertrand de Jouvenel and Harold Lasswell, suffer from a serious drawback for they ignore the ideals of political idealism in their craze for factual insights of political realism. They ignore the elements of free thought, choices, reason, complexity of human behaviour and, above all, the higher forms and aspirations of human life. They forget that 'man's interior world is not a placid realm of saintliness, at present being battered and abused by the forces of giantism; rather, it is a battleground of good and evil, a struggle in which impulses which are squalid, vicious and destructive are locked in an unending battle for mastery with those which are noble, lovely and (dare one say?) divine'.[15] It, therefore, becomes highly essential that, today, social responsibilities ought to be guided by norms and values (derived from all moral disciplines), for the politics in the contemporary period has to move according to 'the ever-changing human relations of a secular culture'.[16] Looking at human nature, it could be asserted that the divorce of morals and values from political theory would seriously cramp and weaken its parameters. One ought to remember that the political man is a much less predictable animal than the economic man and he will remain so. One ought to remember that today is for ever giving birth to tomorrow and tomorrow will necessarily be different, for change is inherent in the process. A process of change can hardly be alienated from values. Morals and values are intertwined with human nature. For unpredictable human nature, a political theory based on the value-fact dichotomy is of little significance.

Secondly, the above definitions of 'politics' ignore some vital dimensions of political studies. The exponents of structural–functional definitions of 'politics' forget that there is another dimension in which a civil society is deeply interested—the enhancement of values and morals for political betterment. It is futile to expect that the aspirations of a society result from biological or mechanical evolution. At the end of the last century, the doughty exponent of evolution, T.H. Huxley, said in a famous lecture: '... the evolution of society is, in fact, a process of an essentially different character from that which brings about the evolution of species ... .', and he later argued, '... social progress means the checking of the cosmic process at every step and the substitution for it of another which may be called the ethical process'. An ethical process is a value process and it is this which is of utmost importance in the fructification of any political theory. Further, politics is much more than a mere accumulation of facts and explanations. Politics is not 'mechanical engineering', it is still a practice that can be compared to the art of cookery.[17] Politics surely is an art, both a performing and creative art. It is an art of an organized polity, in which and by which men may develop a worthy civilization capable of maintaining and constantly improving itself. The realization of form in human life, individual or collective, is a work of artistry. Its one purpose is 'to fuse political purpose and artistic purpose into one whole'. Politics is in part an argument about values between men who agree about some values, but disagree about others. The dialogue is unending because there is no perfect knowledge of justice and every man has to subscribe to his own order of axiological preferences. Politics is also an argument about the future or, more narrowly, about the future consequences of proposed lines of action.[18] In talking about politics, we cannot avoid value judgements. The moral aspects involved in politics are considerations of duty and considerations of prudence and the good concerned in terms of public advantage and gain. It is in this context that a leading behavioural psychologist, B.F. Skinner of Harvard, has attacked what he calls 'the medical analogy' and the prevailing tendency of social science to think of the problems of men in society as the problems of patients needing cures. He says that the only way to build a better life for men is to undertake a wholesale reconstruction of the environment (in which values have their place), since it is environment which determines everybody's state of mind. The 'wholesale reconstruction of environment' is a difficult task in the absence of values. Further, politics is also a practical activity, which is concerned with how we live together collectively, conduct our affairs, make choices, resolve differences and so on, and it necessarily raises moral issues.[19] Politics is a productive interplay of values (supplemented by facts) and it becomes a virile and dynamic activity in which values are cardinal and central. If anyone who tries to understand the practical questions of national policy explores below the surface, he will discover that they are rooted in questions of philosophy.[20] To re-emphasize, tradition and authority are closely linked in politics and political theory. Neither authority nor tradition is unrelated to reason and reasoning; in fact, tradition in particular is often the very basis of reasoning and rational argument.[21] Can there be any rational argument without values? Can reasoning be divorced from values? These questions carry their own answer, for politics is still a refined art, in which the politician is like a 'flute player'. A felicitous union of history and philosophy in political theory is as relevant for us as it was to Aristotle. Political theory, one must remember, is still the search for or inquiry into the nature of the best regime. Political action, which aims at 'either preservation or change, must be guided by some thought of the good as such'. Without values and philosophy, politics cannot carry on merrily. It would not be understood, it would be a practice without conscience and consciousness of the norms. But if the day ever comes when political theory is really dead, the triumph of information over knowledge will be complete—and that will be the saddest day in human history. What Locke once stated in *The First Treatise of Government* is still useful and relevant to us. He enunciated the fundamental issues of political life as well as of political philosophy as follows: "The great question which in all Ages has disturbed mankind, and brought on them the greatest part of those mischiefs which have ruined cities, depopulated countries, and discarded the peace of the world, has been, not whether there be power in the world, nor whence it came, but who should have it."[22] Who should have and use power? This is a perennial question and, unfortunately, it is one that has been relegated to the background. It would be appropriate to plead along with Cicero that 'ethics always comes first',[23] and in any rich and fruitful political inquiry, values and moral obligations go together. It is essential, as Leibniz saw it, that the wise and virtuous rule and devote their efforts to public welfare, not merely to prevent misery, but to promote actual improvement in the material living conditions and the knowledge and virtue of the citizens.[24] If knowledge and virtue are to be promoted in politics, can one do it at the neglect of values? The purpose of politics is political betterment. Political betterment is an inescapably ethical idea, from which values cannot be banished. A mere quest for facts would prove a profoundly disquieting menace to our civilization, for it would jeopardize the values and multi-valued choices that are so essential for building up a preferable society or a worthy civilization.

Values, Reason and Philosophy

Values, reason and philosophy, supplemented by factual knowledge, ought to be the central concern in any political theory. The empirical-scientific theory lays more emphasis on factual knowledge. It is, therefore, based on several false conceptions. It is based, in the first place, upon a false theory of knowledge—that only 'facts' are real. The truth is that universals are as real as facts, and facts can only have meaning in connection with the universals. Secondly, it is based upon a false conception of scientific method. It tends to assume that facts somehow arrange themselves; actually, it is the political scientist who imparts order and meaning to facts by bringing ideas to bear from within his own head. The political scientist, furthermore, must evaluate at the very outset the materials that he believes are important for him to consider. In the third place, it assumes a false relation between the observer and his data—the observer can never be really objective about his data, for he is a part of it. His data are not like atoms, which are inanimate; they are human beings, like himself, and have feelings and emotions, and he must always be sensitive to them. An observer cannot avoid a bias or a point of view, which is ultimately subjective; within limits, of course, he can achieve detachment. And lastly, any random survey of 100 recent doctoral theses based on empirical theory would reveal the energy and skill of 100 young researchers in telling us pigmy findings, which nobody wants to know. What relevance, if any, does the monumental research effort of observing, documenting, counting, measuring, surveying and quantifying, which is coming out like a heap of rubbish under the brand of empirical-scientific theory, have? Has empirical theory been able to answer any of the big questions of the governance of man? Has empirical theory added anything new to what we already knew before? Has empirical theory been successful in formulating the uniformities and regularities of human behaviour? The answer is obvious. Empirical theory is only a name tag to attach to a certain generation of political scientists, whose only ambition in life is to procure fat research projects from foundations and councils.

Eric Voegelin is, perhaps, correct when he indicates four serious drawbacks in empirical-scientific theory. First, empirical theory has no criteria of relevance because such criteria cannot be drawn simply from empirical knowledge. So, its exponents are prone to indulge in trivial investigations, irrelevant to human purposes. Secondly, empirical theory, while striving for neutrality and objectivity, finds it necessary to invent a new, complicated and even ridiculous jargon. Thirdly, in the attempt to eschew values, empirical theory rejects all grounds for evaluation and treats all values as equal. And finally, while professing neutrality, empirical theorists are for the most part partisans of liberal democracy, and their 'neutral' theories are frequently rationalizations for the values and practices of liberal democracy. While empirical theorists try to disagree with such criticism, the point is that in their search for the objective and clinical science of politics, they have given peripheral treatment to values, rationality and philosophy.

Added to these drawbacks of empirical-scientific theory is another relevant phenomenon. How is that empirical theory developed most vigorously in the US, especially after World War II? The views of Tocqueville can perhaps explain this phenomenon to some extent. It is perhaps not relevant to refer to the routine causes of its growth. One major factor, if we apply Tocqueville's views, is that the US had never created any major independent indigenous school of political philosophy. He writes, "America was the country in the world where philosophy is the least studied." Similarly, Norman Jacobson has noted that the idea of a social science as the embodiment of a provocative vision has not been indigenous to political science in the US. A study of the past indicates 'that the genius of American social and political science has been less the cultivation of novel ideas than their domesticator'. Since the American temperament has been unphilosophical (it is more practical and participatory), the logical corollary has been the creation of the empirical-scientific theory. No one can cite any book written in the US, the home of the behaviouralists, which has made an advance on the classics written by Plato,

Aristotle, Aquinas, Hobbes, Locke, Rousseau, Marx and J.S. Mill. To some extent, the American temperament is also responsible for the erosion of values and philosophy from political theory.

In the contemporary period, many political thinkers have objected to the growth of the empirical trend in political theory. Philosophical reasoning, even in the present century, has been of a high order as compared to the sluggish models and concepts formulated by the empirical theorists. No empirical theorist can match the works of scholars such as E.F. Carritt, R.G. Collingwood, L.T. Hobhouse, J.P. Plamenatz, R.H. Tawney, A.D. Lindsay, E. Barker and H.J. Laski. Despite the behavioural attempts to cramp the value-laden theory, it is really heartening to note the creative work done by trans-empiricists and neo-normative thinkers in recent years. The significant history of American political ideas by Vernon L. Parrington, the illuminating analysis of natural law and the relation of property to sovereignty by Morris Cohen, the analysis of the concept of human nature more in keeping with reality by Reinhold Niebuhr, the analysis of ideals by T.V. Smith and Carl Becker, the stimulating discussion of the ideas of freedom by Zachariah Chafee, the penetrating study of the relationship between the public and the governmental process by John Dewey, the probing of Marxian thought by Sidney Hook, the effective criticism of Marxian determinism on the level of governmental policy and international trade by Jacob Viner, the exposure with devastating force of the gap between the profession of equality in ideology and the maintenance of inequality in practice by Gunnar Myrdal, and the study of the claims of authority in American society by Thurmond Arnold are but a few examples that illustrate that normative theory is not dead, and that creativity and values are the cardinal part of any genuine political theory. The question is whether there is a life for scientific theory 'beyond positivism'. Elinor Ostrom suggests that 'we are coming to the end of an era in political science, a slow, whimpering end', which indicates that 'the hoped for cumulation of knowledge into a coherent body of theory has not occurred'. If the foregoing analysis is correct, which it is, it is futile to expect that values, reason and philosophy can be hurled towards the periphery in political theory. One ought to recognize the centrality of values and reason (the power to draw logical inferences, to make deductions, to connect facts with propositions and to connect one proposition with another). One ought to realize that to relegate values to the periphery is most hazardous for the growth of an appreciative and creative political theory. As Aristotle well saw, political theory must deal with the ideal as well as with the real—or actual—world. The tragedy is that the ghost in the mechanical machine or the bugbear of the scientific method has never dared to see the ideal.

The Penury of Ethical Neutrality

The behaviouralists have pressed ethical neutrality as the central concern of political theory. Commenting upon this theme, Arnold Brecht states that the acceptance of the scientific method proposed by behaviouralism implies a type of relativism. The behaviouralists affirm that values and facts are two separate categories and should be kept analytically distinct. In order to be objective, scientific inquiry must be value neutral. Values are permissible in any scientific analysis only to the extent that they determine political behaviour. In other words, political science is a scientific study of politics in its functional aspect and aims at studying political phenomena through empirical methods. Consider Onega's claim that 'the state, after all, is only a machine whose existence and maintenance depend on the vital supports around it'.[25] Such mechanical metaphors, though they have some utility, have created a delusion in political theory. It has nothing new to say, no new world to project. The creations of language would be devoid of sense unless they served the general project of letting new worlds emerge by means of poetry.

The concept of ethical neutrality, on which the empirical-scientific theory is based, has severe drawbacks. First, the exponents of the value free theory have not been able to formulate precise generalizations and uniform models because the nature and scope of politics is so highly flexible that the immutable regularities of the physical world can hardly be traced. Secondly, the value free quest encourages rigid compartmentalization in political theory. It is methodologically a naive view. Thirdly, the value free theory employs the method of experiment—it introduces artificial control and artificial isolation and, thereby, formulates generalizations based on the idea that where circumstances are similar, similar things will happen. Nothing is more dangerous in political theory than this. Of what use are the empirical models in which nothing can repeat itself in precisely the same manner and real novelty is always emerging? All political systems and processes differ so intrinsically from one another and are always changing so fast that micro–macro empirical theories do not have any lasting importance when compared to broad ethical formulations. Fourthly, the subject matter of politics cannot be artificially simplified by the method of experimental isolation. Political life presupposes the mental life of individuals and groups. It is a complex process for which empirical laws can seldom be formulated. And lastly, the value free theory has not been able to fulfil its task of prediction of the political phenomenon. Political predictions and explanations are difficult on account of a peculiar complexity arising from the interconnection between the predictions and the predicted events. Hence, the basic assumptions of the value free theory that it can ultimately become a science capable of prediction and explanation are fragile and weak kneed.

The Moral versus Mechanical Contrivances in Political Theory

One significant issue in political theory is the conflict between moral and mechanical contrivances. Some mechanical and empirical theorists trace the roots of behaviouralism in the writings of Woodrow Wilson, James Bryce, Walter Bagehot and A.L. Lowell. What is relevant here is that these writers, while emphasizing the 'actualities', have never abandoned the moral and value-laden premises of politics. Their social–political inquiries were prompted by both values and facts, based on keen observation and comparison.

In the writings of Woodrow Wilson, one can locate a confluence of values and facts. As early as in 1879 in *Cabinet Government*and certainly in his doctoral dissertation in 1885, *Congressional Government*, Wilson appeared to be an exponent of Walter Bagehot's 'fresh and original method', which, 'if applied to the exposition of our federal Constitution, would result in a revelation'. He asserted that one who looks at the living reality of government would wonder at the contrast to the paper description—he would see in life much that was not in the books and, in the rough practice of government, he would not find the many refinements of literary theory. If one wished to write practically and critically of the government, Wilson declared, he must 'escape from theories and attach himself to facts ... striving to catch its present and to photograph the delicate organism ... exactly as it is today'. Two decades later, in *Constitutional Government in the United States* (1908), Wilson wrote, "Government is not a machine, it is a living thing ... . It is modified by its environment, necessitated by its tasks, shaped to its functions by the sheer pressure of life." Again in 1911, Wilson declared, "I do not like the term, political science. Human relationships, whether in the family or in the State, in the country house or in the factory, are not in any proper sense the subject matter of science. You must not classify men too symmetrically; you must not gaze dispassionately at them with a scientific eye." This last sentence of Wilson, coming after maturity, perhaps, should be taken as a warning by the exponents of the scientific–empirical theory.

Walter Bagehot (1826–77), though familiar with the best scientific and classical thought of his day, started a value-fact confluence method in constitutional interpretation. His most significant contributions to political theory are contained in *The English Constitution* (1867) and *Physics and Politics* (1869). Instead of describing the English Constitution in arid legal terms, he depicted it as a living thing in action and emphasized not the formal structure, but the actual practice of daily political life. It was based on Bagehot's personal observations and not the rigorous classification of data and statistics. His writings led men to realize that the study of government should be 'a study of life', in which values and facts were intertwined. His findings were based on the keen perception of unforeseen consequences, which were fertile with value-laden premises. Although Bagehot looked beyond constitutional fiction into actual function, he never adhered to ethical neutrality.

James Bryce was a keen sighted observer, with a well trained mind and a broad knowledge of history, law and the physical facts of the world, and his studies were much more comprehensive in collecting and analysing the materials for his observational outlook. It was for this reason that Harold Lasswell, the doyen of the behaviouralists, became fond of using Bryce's *American Commonwealth* (1888) as a touchstone for the inadequacies of the old comparative method, regarding Bryce as rich in hypotheses, but lacking in statistical verification for his generalizations. History and observation, combined with practical experience, was most conspicuous in Bryce's work. It was the finest kind of realism, not behaviouralism. Bryce's advice to American political scientists to 'stay close to facts' was, in fact, creative realism. He did not mean that all questions could be solved after the manner of the natural sciences. Bryce was only, very broadly, encouraging the scientific spirit in political science, a spirit in which logic, reason, values, comparisons and observations had a definite role to play.

A.L. Lowell's writings show the finest kind of idealism and realism. As early as in 1889 in *Essays on Government*, Lowell clearly stated his position: "Anyone who attempts to study a carpet loom, or even an ordinary steam engine, when at rest, will find its mechanism hard to understand … The same principle applies to the study of politics, for the real mechanism of government can be understood only by examining it in action." Perceptive observation and realism was Lowell's methodology. He was a man of deep culture, moral earnestness, ideas and values. Even at Harvard, while teaching the students, he would spend half the year on a critical and historical survey of political philosophy from the time of classical antiquity. In his work, *The Influence of Party upon Legislation in England and America* (1902), which the behaviouralists cite for objective statistical influence in political science, Lowell stated emphatically that judgements should be made in the light of certain moral presuppositions. Lowell upheld values and his 'moralistic' insistence that opinion was not desire, and that the great statesman, like the great moral leader, is one who appeals to the higher emotions, to principles and to self-restraint, not to selfishness and appetite, was significant. At the fag end of his life (1931), Lowell wrote to Graham Wallas: "… the more I see of it, the more I am impressed upon the importance of the moral basis as compared with the mechanical contrivances of the reorganization, that the real test of different forms of government is the stamina that they induce." This sentence reflects the summation of Lowell's thought, where ethics and values occupy a central position.

The political blueprints as designed by Wilson, Bagehot, Bryce and Lowell do indicate a preference for moral bases as compared to the mechanical contrivances to be found in political theory. Their realist models were full of insight, vision and scholarship. The basic question before political theorists in the strange new society that is apparently erupting in our midst is whether Lowell is more relevant or the Lasswellian models (based on empirical-scientific propositions). If one special mission of political science is 'to tame the demon of violence and coercion in human affairs', can the Lasswellian models help us progress on this ideal? This mission can be accomplished, not by Lasswell's technical vocabulary and jugglery, but by Lowell's humane and moral political theory. Whether one agrees or not, the point is that the special mission of politics cannot be cultivated by methodological meliorism, moraine statistics, or vainglorious pretence. Mere quantitative and factual knowledge would be inadequate to meet the challenges of culture shock and the more serious future shock. Mere data laden language in political theory would be insufficient to understand the racial segregation and cruelty laden norms of modern politics.

The observation, so often repeated, that our age is richer in knowhow than in know-what is only another way of saying that a map is no substitute for a journey. An age which does not know where it wants to go concentrates on the making of maps, just as, not knowing what it wants to buy, it concentrates on the making of money.[26] The

Lasswellian models and factual knowledge, similarly, are a tranquilizer against the effects of not knowing where to go. The tracks of political theory on which Lasswell proposes to take it are a snare and a delusion. In Lasswell, there is neither ethics, nor hope of progress. If greatest happiness for men consists in the greatest possible abundance of objects suitable for our enjoyment and in the greatest liberty to profit by them, then Lasswell falters badly. If the realization of the unity of mankind is the distant dream of political theory, then Lasswell is redundant. If Condorcet's idea of reason and Rousseau's concept of compassion are meaningful, then Lasswell ought to be thrown away as wreckage. In fact, Lasswell has wrapped political theory in the grave clothes of mechanical models and thereby stunted its multi-valued dimensions. Lasswell's technological models have brought us 'to the end of free fall'. There is a ghost in Lasswell—it is a mechanical ghost. His distorting mirrors provide a wrong view of human nature and of the ends of politics and society. His mechanical frozen models are political theory's nightmares. Political theory has to be liberated from the grisly dance of the Lasswellian models.

The Centrality of Values

The classical dictum of Ivor Brown that 'politics is but ethics writ large', and Immaneul Kant's saying that 'no political theory can ever advance a step further without first paying homage to the principles of morals and ethics', amply demonstrate that values occupy a central position in the nature of political theory. The inadequacy and lack of perspective of value free political and social theory is recognized by many scholars of repute. Gunnar Myrdal writes, "There cannot be value free sociology ... we employ and we need value premises in making scientific observations of facts and in analysing their causal inter-relations ... a disinterested social science is, from this viewpoint, pure nonsense. It never existed, and it will never exist. We can strive to make our thinking rational in spite of this, but only by facing the valuations, not by evading them." Alvin Gouldner, a well known American sociologist, argued that a person engaging in sociology is bound to have certain values and ideologies, or he is no longer a person and becomes some sort of minotaur, a monster with a human body and the head of a bull, or a man-beast, a cleft creature. Similarly, John H. Hallowell has admirably questioned the feasibility of undertaking 'value free, scientifically oriented' inquiry and argued that "the social sciences are not so much in need of new research techniques as of convictions based upon principles ... . A social science that is not committed to the search for freedom and justice has already signed its own death warrant." These observations are equally applicable to political theory.

Political theory ought to be rooted in value premises and factual knowledge ought to supplement its dimensions. The values ought to be at the centre and the factual knowledge or engineering ought to stay at the periphery. Like light and shadow, they may mix and overlap, mingle and intermingle. A value-fact confluence model, where values are pivotal, would, perhaps, be a more relevant style in political theory for the building of a sane society.

Notes

1. H. Eulau. 1963. *The Behavioural Persuasion in Politics* (Mumbai, Vakils, Feffer and Simons Pvt. Ltd) p. II.
2. Ibid. p. 3.
3. N.P. Guild and K.T. Palmer. 1968. *Introduction to Politics* (New York, John Wiley and Sons) pp. 2–3.
4. W.C. Baum. 1970. 'Political Theory', in *Political Science: The Discipline and Its Dimensions,* (ed.) S.L. Wasby (Kolkata, Scientific Book Agency) p. 282.
5. V.V. Dyke. 1962. *Political Science: A Philosophical Analysis* (Stanford, Stanford University Press) p. 107.
6. D. Easton. 1953. *The Political System* (New York, Knopf) p. 129.
7. V.V. Thursby (ed.). 1969. *Contemporary Political Thought* (New York, Holt, Rinehart and Winston) p. 27.
8. B. de Jouvenel. 1963. *The Pure Theory of Politics* (Cambridge, Cambridge University Press) p. 30.
9. H. Lasswell. 1936. *Politics: Who Gets What, When, How* (New York, McGraw Hill).
10. J.R. Lucas. 1967. *The Principles of Politics* (Oxford, Clarendon Press) p. I.
11. Ibid. p. 3.
12. Harold Williams. 1933. *Kant's Political Philosophy* (Oxford, Basil Blackwell) p. 10.
13. D. Tribe. 1967. *100 Years of Free Thought* (London, Elek Books Ltd) p. 7.
14. John H. Herz. 1957. *Political Realism and Political Idealism: A Study in Theories and Realities* (Chicago, University of Chicago Press) p. 226.

15. John Papworth. 1982. *New Politics* (New Delhi, Vikas) p. 361.
16. R. Niebuhr. 1968. *Faith and Politics* (New York, George Braziller) p. vii.
17. M. Oakeshott. 1962. *Rationalism in Politics* (London, Methuen) p. 119.
18. Maurice Cranston. 1973. *The Mask of Politics and Other Essays* (Alien Lane) p. 19.
19. B. Parekh. 1982. *Contemporary Political Thinkers* (Oxford, Martin Robertson) p. ix.
20. L.J. Halle. 1962. *Men and Nations* (Princeton, N.J., Princeton University Press) p. vii.
21. C.J. Friedrich. 1972. *Tradition and Authority* (London, Pall Mall) p. 13.
22. H. Gilden. 1983. *Rousseau's Social Contract: The Design of the Argument* (Chicago, The University of Chicago Press) p. I.
23. J. Higginbotham. 1967. *Cicero on Moral Obligation* (London, Faber and Faber Ltd) p. 14.
24. P. Riley. 1972. *The Political Writings of Leibniz* (Cambridge, Mass., Cambridge University Press) p. 25.
25. J.O. Gasset. 1957. *The Revolt of the Masses* (New York, W.W. Norton) p. 121.
26. G. Vickers. 1970. *Value Systems and Social Process* (Harmondsworth, Penguin Books) p. 214.

6

The Theory-Politics Rapport

One major intellectual style in political theory, right from the classical days to the present day, has been to illuminate and highlight political practice. The theory-politics rapport is an old style, but one that has acquired new dimensions in recent years. This added impetus to the theory-politics relationship is the cumulative result of a long process of evolution, manifest in the historical growth and development of the state. The long series of political revolutions ushered in by the French Revolution in 1789 and carrying over through the nineteenth century was the most immediate factor in the rise of political theorizing about political practice. The industrial revolution, capitalism and the reaction against both these all involved an enormous upheaval in Western society, an upheaval that affected political theories greatly. The fructification of the state under the panoply of Anglo-Saxon liberal traditions, the Marxist-Leninist variety of socialism and the amorphous ideological wrangles in the Third World countries created an urge among political scientists to explore more vigorously the relationship of political theory with political practice. The modern state, as the central mechanism of political power, operating in a labyrinth of political forces and influences, of groups, associations and individuals, has to formulate policies and implement decisions according to the needs and requirements of citizens and society. It is hardly possible nowadays for the ruling elites to ignore political realities and the actualities of the situation before them. Political theory, therefore, has a double task—to conform to reality and to provide imperatives for a future (and probably better) course of action. Interpreted in this sense, the relationship of political theory with political practice is undeniably great.

Secondly, the intellectual forces of enlightenment released rich streams of practical philosophy for the study of the theory-politics relationship. The emphasis on 'reason', 'positivism' or positive philosophy, 'social facts' and, more recently, the dominant elite theories of social change propounded by Vilfredo Pareto (1848–1923) and Gaetano Mosca (1858–1941) all produced a great debate about the theory-politics relationship.

And lastly, the expansion of cities produced a seemingly endless list of urban problems—overcrowding, pollution, noise, traffic—and, correspondingly, increased state activity. The technological products of science began permeating every sector of life and science started acquiring enormous prestige. Political theorists became occupied with science and many wanted to model politics after the successful physical and natural sciences. This led to a new behavioural revolution in the domain of political science and adherence to the methodological rules of the empirico-theoretical systems from which propositions and theories about political practice flowed in a bewildering manner.

It would now be desirable to analyse the relationship of political theory to political practice, with reference to the ideas of Hegel, Marx, Max Weber, Emile Durkheim, Gadamer, Karl Popper and Jurgen Habermas.

II

G.W.F. Hegel (1770–1831) was one of the most outstanding thinkers of the nineteenth century. Hegel indicated the relationship between political theory and political practice in the famous Preface to his book, *Philosophy of Right.* In the Preface, he explained why he was trying to explore the entire course of human history or, as he put it, the march of the world spirit through history. He stuck to one significant point: A political theorist like him who 'thinks about the meaning of the progress of history cannot conceivably be ahead of the time at which he is writing'. This would explain Hegel's fundamental statement that what is 'real is rational and the rational real', that is, what is rational is actual and what is actual is rational. Whatever be the meaning of this phrase as Hegel himself thought it, the impact has been entirely in one direction—to sanctify the existing as good.[1] And it is the unique task of philosophy to comprehend what this is. It is philosophy which enables us to reconcile 'what lies between reason as self-conscious mind and reason as an actual world before our eyes' and 'to recognize reason as the rose in the cross of the present and thereby to enjoy the present, that is the rational insight which reconciles us to the actual'. Probably, the word, 'reason', meant a moral or, at any rate, a normative notion, or the concrete application of rational logical laws. Hegel was trying to say that the sort of thing that is thought at a particular time has a definite relationship to the sort of thing that is happening at that particular time. Hegel's reliance upon reason to solve social and political problems has been so profound that theory and practice 'are in a one-to-one relationship, and this is so even when it is not immediately evident'. In Hegel's Preface to Plato's *Republic,* there is an interesting little discussion in which Hegel argues that at first sight, Plato's *Republic* may look like an ideal, held before the Greek cities as an objective, but it was not so. "Plato's *Republic* is no more than the extrapolation of the fundamental moral structures of the society to which Plato himself belonged. Reason cannot really transcend reality", that is, theory cannot really transcend political practice. This is the point at which another metaphor of Hegel's becomes relevant. Hegel said: "Philosophy cannot actually teach the world anything. Philosophy can merely grasp the substance of the world as it is; and it can be complete, mature, and in itself perfect, only when the world itself has become mature, complete, perfect." The function of philosophy, Hegel said, is merely to explain and not to create. "When philosophy paints its grey in grey, one form of life has become old and by means of its grey, it cannot be rejuvenated but only known. The owl of Minerva takes its flight only when the shadows of evening are fallen." There is no way for a philosopher to be ahead of the world in which he is living. That is the key to unlock the door to political practice. At another place, Hegel wrote that the state is the reality of the moral world: It is the highest and most perfect embodiment of social morality, or rational freedom; it is the incarnation of the spirit of the world; it is the divine idea as it exists on earth. This meant the kind of state (in general terms) in which he was living did mark the highest achievement of mankind and, in many ways, the ultimate stage of human progress. Hegel's theory thus postulates a very strange relationship between political theory and political practice quite apart from the implicit dogmatism or, if one could use the term, 'historicism' of his analysis of world history. For Hegel, political theory is nothing but ideology in a narrow sense of the word. Ideas merely reflect reality as it is. Political theory cannot change or alter things; it has to be intimate to political realities. It cannot be ahead of reality nor can it be apart from it. For Hegel, if theory deserts reality, it becomes, as he puts it, vain and irrelevant. Despite all the scholarship with which Hegel formulated the concept of the 'reasonable and the real', its serious drawback has been the neglect of the probable course of future action, or political practice. Hegel interpreted the history of mankind as the process by which reason comes into its own. This he put it in the form of the apparent paradox: "All that is rational is real."

Karl Marx rejected the appalling conclusions of Hegel and took the exactly opposite view that matter existed independently of and prior to ideas, and that ideas were merely the reflection or embodiment of matter. Hegel proffered the doctrine of wait and see by saying: "The reality proves itself to be the necessary in the course of its development." Marx secularized the Hegelian view, substituting for reason the class struggle for the means of production and by equipping man with this realization of the meaning of history, making of him the master of history rather than its victim, or the victim of Hegel's 'cunning of reason'. The Hegelian dialectic of ideas was thus translated by Marx into a dialectic of interests,[2] and he described his system as dialectical materialism, instead of dialectical idealism. His method was the direct opposite of Hegel. That is the meaning, too, of Karl Marx's remark: "In Hegel's writings, dialectic stands on its head. You must turn it right way up again if you want to discover the rational kernel that is hidden away within the wrappings of mystification."

III

The most conspicuous example of a very close connection between political theory and politics is to be found, of course, in the life and thoughts of Karl Marx (1818–83). In the first place, Marx's basic conceptions, as they took shape in the 1840s, brought together in a single scheme of thought a great part of the politically oriented theory of the preceding half century: the humanist philosophical anthropology of Feuerbach; the ideas of the French socialists, notably the Saint-Simonians; and the analyses of the political economists of the early stages of industrial capitalism. Secondly, in its developed form, Marx's theory came to occupy a preeminent place in social and political thought as a whole and to have a more profound and dramatic direct influence upon the course of political events than any other single body of ideas has ever done. In its social and political aspects at least, the century which has passed since Marx's death deserves to be called the 'century of Marxism'. No thinker in the history of modern political thought has had so direct, deliberate and powerful influence upon the theory and practice of politics as Karl Marx had done.

This leads us to a significant statement of Marx. In the complicated eleventh thesis of his *Theses on Feuerbach,* Marx wrote: "Philosophers have merely interpreted the world in different ways, what matters is to change it." Some critics have given a vicious interpretation of this statement by saying, Let us forget about philosophy, let us forget about social thought, let us concentrate on changing things, never mind what thinkers say! This is a crude literary interpretation and is not the whole truth of Marx's thesis. Evidently, while thinking about Feuerbach, Marx was not trying to say that philosophy is useless. Moreover, he was not trying to abolish the connection between philosophy and reality, the idea of which he had inherited from Hegel. While demonstrating the disruptive character of Hegel's theory, Marx was 'too frightened to apply them openly, in the storm tossed ocean of politics' and, therefore, the cumbrous and heavy Hegelian weapons were 'set afloat in the tranquil inland lake of aesthetic theory'. What Marx really tried to say was that as long as economic, social and political conditions are in some fundamental sense wrong, philosophy is bound to be wrong as well. It is only once social and political conditions have been put right that philosophy can be right as well. The famous words of Proudhon, "I shall destroy and I shall build", far more aptly describe Marx's conception of his own appointed task.

Marx had an abiding faith in the historical inevitability of processes and he himself engaged in political practice. In the eleventh thesis on Feuerbach, Marx is in fact saying that there is a connection between political theory and political practice, but the connection is not as Hegel saw it. It cannot be held that political theory today is right and true because political reality is right and true. On the contrary, political reality is such that it makes political theory wrong, intrinsically wrong; the conditions of capitalist society do not allow a political theory that is right. Marx's personal way out of a Hegelian position turned upside down was the beginning of one particular tradition, which is still a powerful current. This tradition emphasizes the importance of theory and claims there is a sense in which one should be able to say that theory and practice are not twc separate activities, but intertwined in what is called a dialectical relationship. Theory as the recognition of the historical process is practice, and such practice cannot be without theory. What Marx was trying to say is that theory is a part of a process which is as yet unfinished, and not merely the reflection of a completed process. He believed that values could not be contemplated in isolation from facts, but necessarily depended upon the manner in which the facts were viewed. He believed that a correct estimate of the precise balance of forces in the society to which men belong will itself indicate the form of life which it is rational to pursue. He detested romanticism, emotionalism and humanitarian appeals of every kind. His theory did not contain references to moral progress, eternal justice, the equality of man, the rights of individuals and nations, the history of conscience, the fight for civilization and the other dubious political phrases of democratic liberalism; he looked upon these as so much worthless cant, indicating confusion of thought and ineffectiveness in action.[3] His statements that 'traditions of the dead generations weigh like a nightmare on the minds of the living' and 'this frightful parasitic body (immense bureaucratic and military organization of Louis Bonaparte), which surrounds the body of French society like a caul and stops up all its pores' indicate his earnest desire to tune theory to a more action oriented programme in politics. His emphasis on the primacy of economic factors in determining human behaviour, his realism and sense of history, his attack on abstract principles, his demand that every solution be tested by its applicability to the actual situation, his belief in a wholly new social system, and his faith in an orderly, self-directing society towards human emancipation all open a window into the real world of politics and political realism. Marx's theory, therefore, has become a permanent background of civilized thought and politics, for they are the most radical rupture with the traditional ideas of political practice. Marxism is a philosophy of political realism, based on a profound historical sense. It has changed the tenor of man's thought and political practice. Although Marxism may be riddled with ambiguities and inconsistencies, it remains a landmark in the realm of politics and the critical appraisal of any political system in one way or the other.

IV

In Max Weber's political and sociological thought, the relation of theory with politics is treated rather differently from that of Karl Marx. If Marx aimed to bring social science and politics into the closest possible association, Max Weber set out to distinguish and separate them as sharply as possible. That surely is the meaning, in particular, of his two essays on 'Science as a Vocation' and 'Politics as a Vocation'. In 'Science as a Vocation', Weber gave a deeper reason for his distinction between social theory and politics by saying that no amount of scientific inquiry can prove a value judgement, that however hard we try to research or argue a case in the framework of scientific inquiry, this will not enable us to give sufficient reasons for the truth of a value judgement. For that reason, Weber wanted to keep science entirely on one side and politics on the other. In 'Politics as a Vocation', Weber makes a distinction between an 'ethic of conviction', which refers to absolute values and is not prepared to accept any compromises in reality, and an 'ethic of responsibility', which is a moral approach that judges particular situations in a pragmatic fashion, not leaving absolute moral standards totally out of consideration, but at the same time, not letting them govern one's political actions. He argued that politics must of necessity be governed by an ethic of responsibility because if it were governed by an ethic of conviction, it would in fact be unpolitical. Politics is both a passionate and pragmatic exercise. It is not in any sense the application of social or political theory. The two are separate in important respects. Thus, for Max Weber, contrary to Hegel and to Marx, the hiatus between social theory and political practice seems to be almost absolute.

In Weber's conception of politics, unlike that of Marx, he was guided by a well defined point of view, a distinctive value orientation (although some critics associate him with value free dichotomy). Karl Lowith argues that for both these thinkers, the central concern is 'philosophical anthropology' (or the non-empirical conception of men in modern capitalist society), which centres, in Marx's case, upon the idea of 'alienation' and, in Weber's case, upon the idea of 'rationalization'. For Marx, the reference point was the proletariat; for Weber, it was the nation-state. Further, Weber treats the relationship of political theory to practice rather differently from Marx. If Marx aimed to bring social science and politics into the closest possible association, at one place, Weber set out to distinguish and separate them as sharply as possible, while at another place, he argued upon their intimate relationships.

Max Weber's conceptions of politics, political efficacy and political imperatives rest upon five predicates: (a) politics is a realm of power and violence; (b) it is a matter of managing and working in complex organizations; (c) it is a professional, not a vocational sphere, in which the crucial actors are political careerists and entrepreneurs; (d) it is a life of choice and commitment, hence for passionate men; and (e) since its choices are nothing if not systematically implemented, the passionate men must be not mere sentimentalists, but 'men of perspective', who harness ardour to judgement and calculation.[4]

It would be wholly inconsistent with Weber's underlying conception of the social world to suppose that any kind of human activity could be 'value free'. On the contrary, it was a fundamental tenet of his thought that all human action consists precisely of endowing the world with meaning and value. The distinction between science and politics, therefore, is one between two different value spheres, science being the sphere of cognitive values (or what Weber also refers to as rationalization and intellectualization) and politics being the sphere of those values related to struggles for power and the exercise of power (hence also the use of violent means).

More important in the present context, however, is the fact that Weber did not regard the different value spheres as being entirely closed off from each another. On the contrary, in his essay on the meaning of 'value freedom', he sets out plainly his view that it is 'cultural (evaluative) interests (which) give purely empirical scientific work its direction'. Again, in his essay on 'objectivity', he says that there is no absolutely 'objective' analysis of culture or ... 'social phenomena', independent of special and 'one sided' points of view, 'according to which ... they are selected, analysed and organized for expository purposes'. And he concludes this essay with a strong reaffirmation of the influence of extraneous cultural values upon science: "All research in the cultural sciences in an age of specialization ... will regard the analysis of (its) subject matter as an end in itself ... . It will cease to be aware of its rootedness in ultimate value ideas. And it is good that this is so. But a time comes when the atmosphere changes. The significance of the unreflectively used points of view becomes uncertain ... . The light of the great cultural problems has moved on. Then science too prepares to change its standpoint and its conceptual apparatus ... . It follows those stars which alone are able to give meaning and direction to its labours."

Thus, Weber emphasized very strongly the influence of other cultural values upon science; he does not give equal consideration to the reciprocal influence of science upon other values. It seems that Weber assigns the value realm of science to a subordinate place, perhaps his intention was to undermine the Marxian position of the economic interpretation of history by arguing that this is only one possible interpretation among others, equally valid, made from different extraneous value standpoints. By contrast, in his substantive studies of modern capitalism, Weber lays great stress upon the general cultural influence of science as a major element in the process of rationalization, intellectualization and disenchantment of the world. In his essay on 'Science as a Vocation', he makes one brief reference to this phenomenon as the 'fate of our times', while declaring at the same time that he himself 'hates intellectualism as the worst of devils'.

For Weber, social science and political practice are closely interrelated. Science has important implications for practice. This is because it provides some of the necessary empirical foundation for realistic action and policy and for a coherent political standpoint. It by no means provides all this foundation; a good deal is also contributed by the accumulation of experience on the part of politicians, administrators and others, which may be unreflective and unsystematic. But at least one of the characteristics of social science is that it can contribute to effective political practice, both by providing a tool for 'realistic action and policy' and by serving as a weapon against the lack of realism and mistaken assumptions of others.

There is, however, another side to Weber's ideas. His writings are rich in themes that are absent from his sociological work: the struggle for power within society; the development of political leadership; the character of modern democracy; and, the effects of international conflict on national political structures and vice versa. His writings on the politics of Germany and Russia offer an analysis of the interaction between society and the state. Here, for Weber, social science and political practice are 'closely interrelated'. Science has important implications for practice. This is because it provides some of the necessary empirical foundation for realistic action and policy and for a coherent political standpoint. It by no means provides all this foundation; a good deal is also contributed by the accumulation of experience on the part of politicians, administrators and others, which may be unreflective and unsystematic. But at least one of the characteristics of social science is that it can contribute to effective political practice, both by providing a tool for realistic action and policy and by serving as a weapon against the lack of realism and mistaken assumptions of others. He insisted that a correct apprehension of reality was a precondition of successful political practice. Correct empirical analysis was as important for politics as for science; the ability to recognize inconvenient facts as much a virtue in the politician as in the academic. This is pointed out by Von Schelting in what is the most comprehensive analysis of Weber's methodology. The attainment of responsible political action, he writes, '"stands or falls with the possibility of achieving objectively valid knowledge of the empirical relationships pertaining in those areas of social and economic life which are relevant for the standpoint of the actor … . No one knew this better than Max Weber."[5]

A political scientist and a politician, thus, appeared to Weber first in identical, then separable and, in certain senses, even antithetical roles. Even then the desire to join the two in some manner never left him. Aron puts it precisely by saying that in his life and work, Weber 'both separated and united politics and science', a phrase that could serve well as a general characterization of political theory and its practice.

V

The definite theories of Emile Durkheim (1858–1917) constitute another landmark in the domain of political practice. Although primarily a sociologist whose one ardent purpose was the objective study of social facts, Durkheim also had another practical purpose in life that was more closely related to the 'regeneration of France', and to accomplish this aim, he tried to discover 'through science the moral restraint which can regulate economic life'. In brief, Durkheim had two aims—one theoretical, the other, practical.

The most systematic exposition of his definite theories is contained in the *Rules of Sociological Method* (1895), where his emphasis was on the objective study of social facts. This work is an attack on the right of metaphysical doctrine of any variety to exercise an intellectual tyranny over sociology, and an insistence on the ultimate knowability of human action and belief. Here, Durkheim insisted that if sociology really wished to operate scientifically, it should treat its material in the way the natural sciences treated theirs—not introspectively, but as something objective, something which offered itself tangibly to the perception, and it should be recognized and studied only as such. He posed the basic question that the science of society must begin, as does every science, by posing questions; thereafter, one should review and criticize the existing explanations and finally present one's own views, with the supporting evidence. Durkheim, thus, elaborately formulated the rules for the reliable observation, explanation and testing of social facts. He believed that theories try, above all, to be definitive, that is, to be seen to be submitted to carefully designed conditions of test. He strongly insisted upon the practical relevance of theory and on the contribution it could make towards the formulation of a moral code appropriate to the conditions of the new society.

This brings us to the second aspect, the practical purpose of Durkheim's thought. His theories were directed towards the creation of a new society; he knew that the task of conceptualizing and achieving a new society was no easy one. He wrote: "We know only too well what a laborious work it is to erect this society where each individual will have the place he merits, will be rewarded as he deserves, where everybody, accordingly, will spontaneously work for the good of all and of each." His primary aim was to discover and implement a new moral regulation of society (in social and political conditions) and the construction of social science was subordinated to this end. Durkheim's concern with morality seems to have become increasingly prominent in the last year of his life, when he began to write a book on morality, which was 'the purpose of his existence and the foundation of his thought'. His idea of moral regulation had a political sense. In Durkheim's work as a whole, unlike that of Marx and Weber, there is relatively little direct analysis of political power. Only in the course of some lectures given in the 1890s did Durkheim formulate, in brief, his conception of the state as "a special organ responsible for elaborating certain representations which are valid for the collectivity. These representations are distinguished from other collective representations by their higher degree of consciousness and reflection ... Strictly speaking, the state is the very organ of social thought." For Durkheim, the state is the 'supreme moral regulator of society', it 'embodies and expresses a national collective will', and 'has primacy over all other interests and purposes in society'. He rejected the idea of working class internationalism, the Marxian class struggle appeared to him as a temporary (and, of course, undesirable) 'abnormality', and he emphasized a reformed educational system to provide adequately to the young generation the moral education that would equip them for their tasks in the collective life of the nation. These ideas of Durkheim about the new society, the State and morality place him in the ranks of a social idealist.

Although Durkheirn's political commitment was very similar to that of Max Weber, it developed in different circumstances and so took a different form. Where for Weber, the political problem consisted in maintaining or reviving the impetus given to German expansion by the unification of Germany under Bismarck, for Durkheim, the problem was to recreate a powerful and stable French nation-state in the conditions resulting from defeat in the war with Prussia and violent class antagonisms and to provide a secure foundation for the Third Republic. Both Weber and Durkheim were guided in the elaboration of their theories by their commitment to a strong nation-state, based upon capitalist production (though this was to be in some sense a reformed capitalism in which welfare provisions would allay class antagonisms) and modern in the sense that it would be a democratic state (though this conception was qualified in Weber's case by the notion of the 'plebiscitarian leader' and was not fully analysed by Durkheim).

There were, of course, some important differences between Weber and Durkheim. Durkheim did not assert, as Weber did, that the interests of the nation-state constitute an absolute standard of value. On the contrary, in his brief analysis of the state, he referred explicitly to values common to humanity as a whole, which were 'higher' than those of any particular nation, although he placed the actual embodiment of such values in social institutions in a very distant and uncertain future and so concluded that for the time being, such values could only be expressed by nation-states. Undoubtedly, though, Durkheim was a more moderate nationalist than was Weber and we might say, in a general comparison of their political commitments, that Durkheim was more liberal and democratic than Weber, but also less of a realist in the sense that his concept of the state as a moral agency largely excluded recognition of its character as an instrument of power and violence.

VI

The contemporary debate about the theory-politics relationship revolves around three major themes: first, of a hermeneutical approach to society and politics; second, of an objectivist and piecemeal engineering approach; and third, of a dialectical–critical approach. Gadamer is the advocate of the first, Popper of the second, and Habermas of the third.

One of the most important and lucid interpreters of hermeneutical theory in modern times has been the German philosopher, Hans-Georg Gadamer, whose major work, *Truth and Method* (1960), has strongly influenced subsequent discussion. Hermeneutical theory has been considerably influenced by work in aesthetics, as well as biblical interpretations, and psychoanalysis—all areas in which the development and explication of interpretive theories have been central. Gadamer's main concern was understanding how this was possible. He wrote, "The central question of the modern age, viz., how our natural view of the world—the experience of the world that we have as we simply live our lives—is related to the unassailable and anonymous authority that confronts us in the pronouncements of science." He criticized the way in which 'natural' unreflective aesthetic and historical forms of consciousness had become alienated through striving for objective judgements about art and history; he hoped to show that 'it is not so much our judgements as it is our prejudices that constitute our being'. The concept of prejudice had to be rehabilitated: "Prejudices are not necessarily unjustified and erroneous, so that they inevitably distort the truth. In fact, the historicity of our existence entails that prejudices, in the literal sense of the word, constitute the initial directedness of our whole ability to experience. Prejudices are biases of our openness to the world. They are simply conditions whereby what we encounter says something to us." Thus, people are open to the world—in a state of questioning or 'hermeneutical conditionedness'—and this is a universal state, for the scientist as much as for the artist or for anyone else. It is the asking of new questions, not scientific methodology, which leads to new knowledge, and this is the hermeneutical element of all experience, including science. It is this element which joins science and life experience together and reveals, in Gadamer's view, the fundamental level of the 'linguistic constitution of the world'. One must understand the world (or political practice) through an insight of historical consciousness and particularities, which, of course, is a process of constituting the world through language. Our consciousness of the world is affected by history and fulfilled by language. A hermeneutical interpretation distinguishes the false from the true prejudices that illuminate the text of history. This interpretive tradition is deep rooted in

German tradition, and called Geisteswissenschaft (science of the mind or culture). The key words in hermeneutical theory about politics are interpretive, linguistic and historical consciousness. It is only through the interpretative approach that the knowledge of political practice can be enhanced.

The second contemporary approach to the nature of human studies and their relationship to natural science is that of Karl Popper, a leading exponent of the analytical tradition. He has written widely on the philosophy of science and the relationships of scientific method and understanding to the solving of social problems. The crux of Popper's thesis is: (a) "The method of science is one of tentative attempts to solve our problems by conjectures which are controlled by severe criticism. It is a consciously critical development of the method of 'trial and error'; and (b) The so called objectivity of science lies in the objectivity of the critical method. This means, above all, that no theory is beyond attack by criticism, and further, that the main instrument of logical criticism—the logical contradiction—is objective."

Closely related to this basic conception of Popper's were several other important ideas. First, while he accepted that no science—natural or social—could be separated from the extra-scientific interests and values that influenced it, he tried to draw a distinction between those values and the values of scientific enquiry itself. No scientist could be free from cultural values, but he should strive to uphold the scientific values of truth, relevance, simplicity and so on, attempting to separate the two realms of value. Secondly, it is thus the value commitment and task of pure science, including social science, to search for objectively true causal explanations. The standard of truthful causal explanation should become the regulative principle of a critical scientific procedure. Thirdly, social science should conform to the methodological prescription as much as natural science. A purely objective social science was possible, he believed, if it employed the method of objective understanding. Finally, history has no intrinsic meaning, but it could be given a meaning through making a conscious decision to do so. Historical facts and decisions about meaning had to be rigorously separated. This was the failure of 'historicism', which he styled as a kind of fatalism. Against this historicism, Popper proposed for social science a piecemeal technological purpose which rested upon an instrumentalist view of social theory. The task of the social engineer was to 'design social institutions, and to reconstruct and run those already in existence' in accordance with certain decided ends. The piecemeal engineer never aims to remodel the whole of society. It is not a holistic approach. It lays emphasis on an open mind as to the scope of the reform, rejects *a priori* hypotheses, and admits the importance of tests and the principles of scientific method. "Without the possibility of tests, any claim that a scientific method is being employed evaporates. The holistic approach is incompatible with a truly scientific attitude." Thus, the empirical testing of theories, the fact–value distinction with science, the unification of natural and social scientific methods and the rejection of holism can be styled as Popper's model for the study of political practice.

Another important political thinker was Jurgen Habermas, the chief inheritor of the Frankfurt School of political thought, which developed from the 1920s. He was a leading antagonist of Popper's positivism. The Frankfurt School derived its themes from the more Hegelian and dialectical elements in Marxism as well as from other traditions of German philosophy. It aimed to develop a critique of alienation, which lies at the heart of capitalist culture with its scientific–technological rationality. From the 19960s onwards, Habermas has attempted to unite a hermeneutical conception of social experience and understanding with the desire for an objective and emancipating basis for social knowledge and sociopolitical practice. To achieve this aim, he has criticized boldly both the German hermeneutical tradition and the predominantly Anglo-American analytical- positivist tradition. Habermas's objections to positivism (and hence to Popper) were significant. First, he rejected any analytical distinction between theory on the one hand, and its object, experience, history or practice on the other. He asserted the importance of a dialectical (or mutually interacting) and hermeneutical unity of theory and social reality. Second, he said that theory should be construed in the context of an actor's prior experiences and pre-understandings of a social totality and should then be checked by the theorist against his own experience in a dialectical manner. Third, according to him, it was insufficient to adopt either a subjectivist hermeneutical approach or a causal–analytical approach. He wished to transcend both hermeneutics and causal–analytical science by confronting the real with the possible, that is, by having a transformative intention. A practical theory must be critical of the social totality. Fourth, the technological attitude has the effect of eliminating questions about genuine life practices from social science. A dialectical attitude alone can draw attention to the gaping discrepancy between practical questions and merely technical tasks. The motivation and legitimization of social science should be the solving of the problems of the overall practice of life itself, rather than decisions about the implementation of manipulative 'corrections'. Habermas thus developed the concept of a critical theory—one that is able to transcend both interpretative understanding and technical control by having an emancipatory intent. For Habermas, the emancipation of socialized man from the ideological and technical control of the modern state and of the international political and market systems was and should be the goal of all critical political theorists.

VII

We have thus discussed some of the significant political theories relating to political practice. They contain divergent, sometimes overlapping, but always important viewpoints. No one theory can be styled as a final dictum in the domain of political practice, nor is this possible. Hegel's dialectical idealism is no doubt important, but his concept of 'reasonable and the real' neglects the probable course of future action. His view that the function of philosophy is to explain and not to create contains only half the truth.

Marx, in opposition to Hegel, boldly proclaimed that a mere interpretation of the world on the basis of philosophy was not enough, the point is to change it. Here, he grasped the meaning of political practice; if the existing practice is wrong, it has to be altered. His elaborate scientific structure, built on the theme of economic determinism, is indeed a remarkable piece of political theory, aiming at change in the exploitative social order. Whatever Marx might have thought, his ideas have given birth to a new political and administrative structure of a society based on the principle of 'democratic centralism', a principle starkly simple, yet beguilingly vague.

The ideas of Max Weber, as contained in his essays on 'Science as a Vocation' and 'Politics as a Vocation', plead a dichotomy between theory and practice. They become dangerous for they widen the gap between theory and practice. What is required is to expose the two to each other. Political practice should be continually argued and political theory should take into account the experiences of political practice. The theories of Emile Durkheim in which he strove hard to discover 'through science the moral restraint which can regulate economic life' are indeed fascinating, but his concern with morality and the creation of a new society have never seen the light of day. They have the power of illumination, but lack the energy of science.

The hermeneutics of Gadamer could lead to political passivity—concentration simply upon understanding actors' perceptions, rather than upon explaining the structural imperatives and constraints of action. A Popperian objectivist and decisionist philosophy leads to piecemeal social engineering for technical rather than liberating ends. And Habermas's critical theory will lead not to utopianism (as Popper believed), but to the potential for democratic control of the structures of everyday life made possible by uncovering them from beneath their ideological disguises.

With this sketchy evaluation of the political theories of political practice, perhaps, one final word is essential regarding the meaning of political theory and its possible relationship with political practice.

VIII

Today, political theory is in a state of uneasiness. Its field has become a mausoleum of names and doctrines, of authorities and dogmas. There is no finality about its meaning, scope and purpose. Notions are widespread that it is either an industrious activity on the drawing boards of architects of fantasy, or a branch of esoterics operating in a shadowy realm. There are, to borrow Nietzsche's terms, Apollonian and Dionysian conceptions of political theory. Favourite descriptive adjectives for theory by persons holding the Apollonian conception are 'abstract', 'grand' and 'large-scale'. To them, it appears, theory is an odyssey through the utopian islands of make-believe, with an occasional detour up the spiral staircase of an ivory tower. On the other hand, favourable descriptive adjectives for theory by persons holding the Dionysian interpretation are 'elusive', 'obscure' and 'ephemeral'. To them, it seems, theory is a dangerous if exhilarating business, in which one makes one's way along the rat infested waterfronts of the human spirit.

Neither of these conceptions truly reflects the meaning of political theory. If theory is to be compared to anything, it can most probably be a light. As far as possible, theory has only one function—to illuminate and to explain. The difference between one theory and another is in comparative candle power. The power and reliability of theory are not always evident all at once. A theory may have the power to explain what was not originally anticipated; it may also disclose the existence of problems it cannot explain. The inevitable process is of attempting to improve a theory and of searching for alternatives to it. Theory is both a philosophy and a science; the task of the former is to illuminate and the task of the latter is to explain. A mere emphasis on science, or 'theory as a tool', contains only the partial truth. Its proponents think it but 'an easy leap to pluck bright honour from the pale-faced moon'. The point is that a mere explanation based on terminological pyrotechnics or scientific data would miss the real illuminating power of theory. The importance of theory lies, not in the extension of scientific tools and techniques, but in the generalization of the scientific programme, co-extensive with political thought itself. Theory requires a cooperation of reason (normative) and energy (science). Such a theory alone can help us to illuminate and to explain political practice.

Lytton Strachey, in one of the portraits of historians, remarked that three qualities make a historian, for absorbing facts, a capacity for stating them, and a point of view', and he continued: "The latter two are connected, but not necessarily inseparable." The late Professor Samuel Gardiner, for instance, could absorb facts and he could state them, but he had no point of view; the result is that his book on the most exciting period of English history resembles nothing so much as a very large heap of sawdust. Similarly, the landscape of political theory is abundantly furnished with heaps of sawdust, large and small. But this is not all that it contains. Those thinkers who mapped the territory, invented the concepts, sketched the hypotheses and theories, such as Hegel, Marx, Durkheim, Weber, Gadamer, Popper and Habermas, had the capacity to absorb facts, the capacity to state them, and a point of view, one that was pre-eminently sociopolitical. A 'point of view' may be a quest for truth, reality, idealism, emancipation and sociopolitical betterment. Political theory, therefore, is nothing more than a 'point of view' about existing political practice and its future manifestations. Such a 'point of view' can have varied shapes and dimensions, depending upon the flexibility of politics and the pliability of human nature. One must remember that the realities of political practice are such that they do not lend themselves to being organized and controlled through any fixed theory. Although theoretical reflection about politics is important, it cannot be wholly unified with practice because of a fundamental variation in their interests and ethics. Theory is at its best an indicator, an illumination, an explanation or a clue to the understanding of politics. It is, to a great extent, a mere derivation of cultural values and social and economic conditions. It offers a measuring rod by which one can evaluate political performance, anticipate happenings and develop images of the future. If one says that all political practice has to be theoretical, then one ignores the realities of politics, the pressures which exist, the institutions which constrain action, the needs of power, and so on. In other words, to construct a bridge between political theory and political practice is perhaps an intricate task because the gap between theory and practice has always existed and, probably, will always continue to exist.

Notes

1. William Ebenstein. 1960. *Modern Political Thought: The Great Issues*, 2nd edition (New Delhi, Oxford and IBH Publishing Co.) p. 323.
2. Kurt H. Wolff. 1974. *Trying Sociology* (New York, John Wiley and Sons) p. 75.
3. Isaish Berlin. 1978. *Karl Marx: His Life and Environment* (Oxford, Oxford University Press) pp. 7–8.
4. Harry Eckstein. 1967. 'Political Science and Public Policy', in *Contemporary Political Science: Toward Empirical Theory,* (ed.) Ithiel de Sola Pool (New York, McGraw Hill Book Co.) p. 135.
5. David Beetham. 1974. *Max Weber and the Theory of Modern Politics* (London, George Allen and Unwin Ltd) pp. 250–51.

Index